# THE HOME GYM

# A GUIDE TO FITNESS EQUIPMENT

# THE
# HOME
# GYM

# A
# GUIDE
# TO
# FITNESS
# EQUIPMENT

# MICHAEL LAFAVORE

AVON
PUBLISHERS OF BARD, CAMELOT, DISCUS AND FLARE BOOKS

**THE HOME GYM: A GUIDE TO FITNESS EQUIPMENT** is an original publication of Avon Books. This work has never before appeared in book form.

AVON BOOKS
A division of
The Hearst Corporation
1790 Broadway
New York, New York 10019

First Avon Printing, September, 1984

AVON TRADEMARK REG. U. S. PAT. OFF. AND IN
OTHER COUNTRIES, MARCA REGISTRADA, HECHO EN
U. S. A.

Printed in the U. S. A.

DON 10 9 8 7 6 5 4 3 2 1

To Laura, for the lost weekends

# CONTENTS

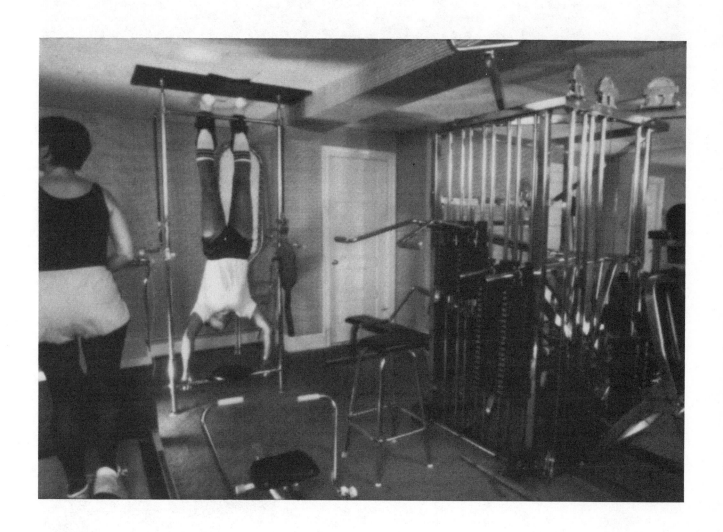

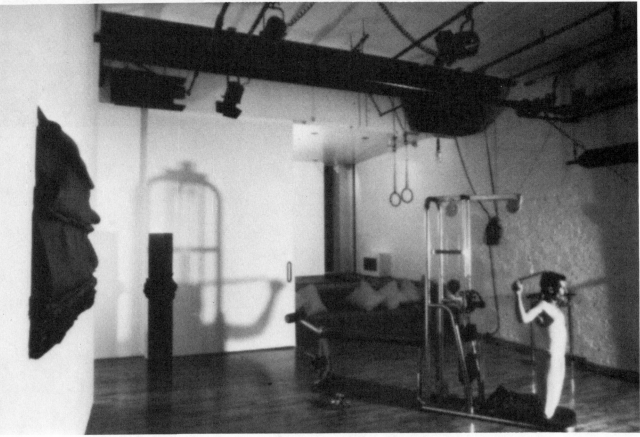

# PART

# I

# THE
# BASICS

# 1

## A SPA AT HOME

Cheryl Tiegs has one. So do Clint Eastwood, Morgan Fairchild, Kris Kristofferson, Robert DeNiro, Linda Evans, Billy Dee Williams, Barbara Carrera, Neil Diamond, Connie Stevens, John Travolta, Linda Ronstadt, Charlton Heston and Jack LaLanne. Sylvester Stallone keeps his out by the pool. Calvin Klein has one at the office and another at his apartment.

What do all these celebrities have in common, besides Mercedes? Home gyms. In businesses where staying trim and youthful means staying alive in the popularity polls, they know the benefits of keeping their fitness equipment close at hand. The ultimate Beverly Hills status symbol used to be your own projection room. Now it's a room full of Nautilus machines. Just look at the difference between Stallone in *Rocky* and *Rocky III* to see what regular workouts have done for him. He dropped from a beefy 195 pounds to a lean and mean 155 with a program of aerobics and weight training.

You don't have to be rich, or famous, to have a gym of your own at home. I've got one, too, even though I don't have my own fan club; I know it pays to look and feel as good as I can.

I can sum up my reasons for investing in my own equipment in a word: convenience. It's hard enough work staying in shape without having to deal with a lot of hassles just to get to a gym. I learned a long time ago that a fitness program that isn't easy to live with is one that isn't going to stick.

Perrier, the French mineral water company, recently commissioned Louis Harris and Associates to poll Americans about their attitudes toward fitness. One of the questions they asked was "What would you say are the main reasons that you aren't getting enough exercise?" The largest number of respondents, 47 percent, answered "Not enough time." Other reasons given were "the weather" (15 percent) and "family obligations" (19 percent).

I wish I'd read that a few years ago, before I joined a commercial health club. Even though the statistics say there are 5,000 clubs out there, it figured that the nearest one to *my* house was six miles away. I knew I needed the exercise, so I ignored the distance at first and signed up.

Like most people, I paid my first year's dues in advance and promised myself I'd get my money's worth. And I did, at least for a few months. It took about that long for me to realize that the times when I wanted to work out were the same as the hours that just about every other member wanted to. Between 6 and 9 P.M. the place looked like the Times Square subway station. The lines of people in front of all the best equipment snaked halfway across the room. I found myself doing lots of socializing with the people queued up around me, but not as much exercising as I should have.

Then one week it snowed. And another week the car was in the shop. Then I had to work late. The excuses got progressively feebler: no clean clothes, a good mini-series on TV, broken shoelaces on my sneakers. In the end I quit bothering to even think up excuses. The workouts had become too infrequent to do me any good, so I stopped going to the gym altogether. My well-intended experiment with health clubs wound up costing me about $150 a month.

The clubs are fine for some people, mainly those with very flexible temperaments and schedules. But for a lot of us, dealing with aggravations like long drives in bad weather, long lines at the clubs, babysitters, lack of privacy, and traveling home in the cold with our hair still wet from a shower, make the entire experience just too much bother. Perhaps that's why, according to the *New York Times,* only about 20 to 25 percent of the members of many clubs renew for a second year.

Like me, Marilyn Kriegel of Mill Valley, California, is a health-club refugee. A professor of holistic studies at Antioch University, she set up her own gym at home several years ago.

"I work long, unpredictable hours, and it's hard to make time to schlepp over to a health club unless it's open until 11 or 12 at night." Now her exercise program starts when she rolls out of bed at 6 A.M. Most days she heads straight for her multi-station weight unit on the other side of her room. Once there, she works her way through half a dozen exercises designed to strengthen her arm, leg, stomach and back muscles.

Next, she'll wander into the den, put something eye-opening on the stereo and climb aboard her stationary bike. She spends the next 20 minutes pedaling away while flipping through a magazine or *The New York Times Book Review* placed on the reading rack attached to her bike. If the weather's nice, she often ends up out on the sun deck, bouncing on her mini-trampoline while watching the waves slip onto the northern California shore.

After her morning exercise regimen, Marilyn feels ready to take on a long day at her job. "Working out gets my energy level up and at the same time it's calming, like meditation," she says. "I wouldn't be nearly so relaxed if I had to go through a lot of bother before and after."

Having your own health club at home won't make doing your exercises any easier. There's still no substitute for sweat. But equipping your home for fitness will surely make your exercise sessions more convenient. You can forget about other people's schedules and tailor your fitness program to your own best hours. And when you can subtract travel time from the equation, staying fit takes less of those hours.

The benefits of home gyms don't end with convenience. For me, another big advantage is privacy. It isn't that I'm not a social person, it's just that I prefer to grunt and sweat on my own and meet friends later. And if my legs are white or my T-shirt is a bit shabby, who's to know?

My gym is also a personal space—one I designed to fit my own tastes and needs. The "Early Mall" decor, orange carpet and fluorescent lights at the health club just weren't my style. I prefer soft, relaxing colors and track lighting.

With a gym at home, excuses for not exercising are hard to come by. Guilt is a great motivator. When the health club is miles away, it's easy to think of a reason not to go and forget about it. But when the equipment you paid good money for is sitting right in the next room and you have to look at it sitting forlorn and unused every time you walk by, it's a constant reminder that you could be exercising. If you really want to stay fit, that gentle mental nudge is all it usually takes.

The lure of a home gym isn't always a negative tug on your guilt strings. When you walk into the house after a rough day out in the world, your gym will look like a very inviting oasis. You'll be amazed at how fast you can work away those anxieties and aggressions by pounding your own punching bag for 15 minutes (with the photo of your choice pasted on the front) or pedaling a few miles on your stationary bike. It sure beats taking it out on the kids.

And speaking of children, what better way for them to make fitness a lifetime commitment than to grow up with a gym at home? Two years ago, Dr. Wynn F. Updike of Indiana University's School of Health surveyed the results of fitness tests given to

7,600 youngsters from across the country. He found that fewer than half of the children were able to meet fitness standards that should be attainable by the average healthy young person. Surprisingly, he discovered that as kids get older, their physical fitness actually declines. For example, the average 15-year-old boy in the study took 13.3 seconds to sprint 100 yards, while the average 14-year-old boy could do it in 12.6 seconds. The typical 17-year-old girl could do only 38 modified push-ups in 2 minutes, while the average girl 5 years younger could do 42 in the same amount of time.

"Clearly there is room for improvement," said Dr. Updike, commenting on the results of his study. "The fitness and conditioning habits of a lifetime are formed in childhood, and America's habits are not all they should be."

That's where you come in. Children learn many of their future habits, good and bad, from their parents. The vast majority of smokers, for example, grew up in a house where one or both parents smoked. If they see Mom and Dad exercising regularly and staying fit, they'll know it's worthwhile and important and will want to emulate them. If the schools are failing to get and keep kids fit, as Dr. Updike's study would imply, then maybe you should hold your own "gym class" at home and make it a fun, family activity.

You can start an informal kiddie exercise program when your children are still very young. If you have mats on your gym floor, encourage toddlers to roll, bounce, slide and kick their feet. Before age three, youngsters seem to respond to this unstructured activity. So if there's nothing nearby for them to bang into, just let them wail around the gym while you work out.

When the kids get a little older they may enjoy bouncing on your mini-trampoline. Just stay close by, because their coordination may not be fully developed yet. If you have a swimming pool, bring the kids in with you when they're young and hold them while they kick their feet and splash with their hands.

A weight-lifting program really isn't necessary until after children reach puberty. Studies have demonstrated that before puberty there is little strength or muscle size to be gained from weight training. The reason seems to be a shortage of adult hormones.

If you own a multi-gym unit or pulley-type weight machine there's no harm in letting 10- or 11-year-olds use it with supervision, provided you can adjust the weight to very light loads. Start children off with no more weight than they can lift 5 times without tiring, and don't let them increase it until they can lift it at least 10 times in a row.

Free weights are risky business in the hands of children and young teenagers. Accidents can, and do, happen even with the special scaled-down barbells made for kids. According to the Consumer Products Safety Commission, over half the weight-lifting injuries that occurred in 1979 were in 10- to 19-year-olds. If your son or daughter wants to work with free weights, make sure it's with light loads and that there's always an adult "spotter" close by to grab the weights if the child slips.

A home gym is a great place for kids and adults to stay in shape for sports. During the winter a lot of us let ourselves get a bit soft around the edges and then it's a hard, uphill push to get ready for the sports season. Professional athletes know that, which is why people like Gerry Cooney, Sugar Ray Leonard, Bruce Jenner and Mark Gastineau of the New York Jets have built private gyms for themselves. But even if you only want to improve your arm to pitch for the company softball team, or keep in shape for a weekly bout of handball with a friend, regular workouts can't help but improve your game.

If bicycle touring or racing is your passion, a stationary bike should be standard equipment for winter training. Just make sure you find a good one,

with adjustable resistance to prepare you for those hills out in the real world. Bikers should also work on their upper bodies with weights. Developing strength and flexibility in the arms, neck, buttocks and back will help you ride longer and harder without tiring.

Racquet sports demand strength and endurance in your arm, shoulder, back, leg and stomach muscles. You can train with weights, lifting relatively light amounts for lots of repetitions. All the racquet sports require cardiovascular fitness— squash and racquetball more so than tennis.

Joggers and indoor treadmills are a natural marriage. On a treadmill, runners can log their weekly miles whether the weather cooperates or not. Again, adjustable resistance is important to simulate actual running conditions as closely as possible. For total fitness, joggers should also concentrate on upper-body strength, an area on which jogging has little effect.

To become the star player

of your baseball or softball team, you'll have to work on increasing strength and power in your arms, back and abdomen to improve your hitting, and your legs for those quick sprints around the bases. Jumping rope will not only give your heart and lungs a needed workout, but can also improve speed, flexibility, balance and eye-hand coordination. And don't forget a regular program of stretching exercises. A lot of the muscle injuries to baseball players occur when they force too-tight leg muscles into sudden action after a hit.

Sometimes it seems that just surviving a punishing day at work takes more energy and stamina than running a marathon. As the day progresses, most of us find ourselves lagging a bit, especially after lunch when our bodies seem to be telling us they would prefer a nap to another meeting.

A noon exercise break, far from sapping your needed energy, will give you a boost, smooth out your frazzled nerves and sharpen your concentration for the rest of the day. It won't take a lot of time; a half hour to 45 minutes three times a week is plenty. Skip the big, calorie-laden lunch for a workout and a salad or soup.

Exercise programs work best when they follow the path of least resistance. If you and enough of your co-workers find it more convenient to work out at lunch, or right before work, talk to your company about putting some equipment in. A corporate gym doesn't have to be as big as the 10,000-square-foot facility at General Foods's headquarters. It's always great when a company puts that kind of money and conviction behind employee fitness, but realistically, an unused conference room or part of the basement with some basic equipment is a step in the right direction.

If the decision-makers aren't entirely won over by your personal zeal, hit them with some cold financial facts. Mention that after the huge Pratt & Whitney company built an office gym and started its own fitness program, its costs for employee health claims dropped—this during the same period when the national cost of medical care went up 12 to 15 percent.

If there's concern in your company about losing valuable, experienced executives to retirement, inform them that 30 percent of the people who retire each year do so not because they want to, but because they are ill or disabled.

Finally, cite the recent studies that show that regular exercise brings on marked improvement in short-term memory, reaction time and problem-solving ability. In short, an investment in employee fitness will pay for itself many times over.

## THE DESIGNER GYM

Most companies would hire consultants and designers to plan a corporate gym. Most of *us* can't afford to do that for a home gym. There's certainly nothing wrong with acting as your own interior designer, provided you start out with an understanding of the basics.

The first decision you'll have to make is where to set up your gym. If Junior is headed off to college soon, your problem is solved; he can sleep on a fold-out couch when he's home on visits. Or evaluate honestly how often the guest room gets used. Even if you entertain a lot and use it 20 days a year, that's 345 days when the guest room can be put to better use.

The next logical places to look for gym space are in the basement or garage. Once you've cleared away the rusting ping-pong table and old snow tires, you'll be left with a raw space begging to be put to good use. All it takes to transform that space into your own private fitness sanctum are some inexpensive partition walls to set aside the section you want to use. As tempting as it might be to skip the cost of the carpenter and set up the equipment among the half-empty cans of paint, spend the few extra dollars and make a special room. Pleasant surroundings are as important to a fitness program as the equipment used.

Take a long look at your living room. Consider giving the words a new meaning. Most living rooms are just places to sit, often used only when company comes. Is that really the best use of what's usually the largest room in the house? If there's another place, like a den, to hang out in, why not "donate" the living room to yourself as a fitness center? When you're done setting up your exercise equipment, there'll probably still be plenty of space for a couch and coffee table. Think of the equipment as part of the decor, oversized conversation pieces.

"Why not put fitness machines out in the open and make a statement about yourself?" asks Kevin Walz, a New York interior designer. "I think a lot of the equipment looks great—like modern chrome sculpture. It's no more out of place in a living room than a television set."

Eric Bernard, another New York designer, gets lots of requests from clients who want home gyms. His favorite suggestion is to expand the bathroom and turn it into a spa. In fact, he dislikes the name bathroom and prefers to call it a "personal retreat."

"Bathroom is such an old-fashioned term," Bernard says. "It implies a room with a very limited use. I like to put in a Jacuzzi or sauna, along with gym equipment and even a good stereo system. Then you've got a rejuvenation center, someplace to go and wash away the tensions of the day when you get home."

Even if a gym in your bathroom—personal retreat—is out of the question, be creative. One Philadelphia couple cut a hole in the ceiling of their bedroom and installed a spiral staircase leading to an attic gym. A New York artist cut a hole in the floor of his loft for a hot tub and hung acrobatic rings from exposed water pipes under his ceiling.

There's no need to let lack of space keep you from having your own gym. Even the most cramped apartments usually have a closet or two. That's all it takes. Get yourself some roll-up mats, and shop for equipment that folds flat when you're not using it. A lot of companies are making folding equipment, everything from stationary bikes to weight machines to inversion devices. A whole gym's worth will fit in a 4-by-4-foot space.

## SWEATING THE DETAILS

A home gym that's functional and fun to be in is more than just a space and some equipment. It's the little details, the way you put things together, that will make it a welcoming place in your home, one that you'll enjoy going to frequently.

Mirrors will create the illusion of a larger space, especially if they cover the walls that face you as you're entering the room. As well as being decorative, mirrors serve several useful functions in a home gym. They allow you to watch yourself as you exercise, so you can check your body position and correct any errors. They also let you watch yourself getting slimmer and trimmer by the week. Large, plate-glass mirrors are heavy and expensive. Stick-on mirrored tiles are much cheaper and easier to install.

Color is a very subjective thing, but quite a bit of research has gone into the moods that various hues bring out in people. Interior design schools even offer courses in the psychology of color. Bright oranges and reds are aggressive colors, not very conducive to relaxation. (Fast-food restaurants, it's said, use these colors so you'll eat in a hurry and vacate your seat for the next customer.) Blues, greens and earth tones are supposed to be more relaxing. Eric Bernard covered the walls of one gym he designed with black leather for a heavy macho look. Before you choose a color for your gym, give some thought to the feeling it brings out in you and how it relates to your attitude about exercising.

I don't care much for fluorescent lighting, and particularly not in gyms.

It's too bright and drains away all the colors in a room, besides giving your skin a sickly, jaundiced cast. Track lighting and individual spots create pools of light, which I find much more pleasant and soothing. With a modular lighting system and dimmers, you can bring the light up when you're using the equipment and tone it back down later to deemphasize its presence in the room. If, for example, the gym equipment is in a bedroom, you can use lights to accent the equipment when you're working out and make it recede into the background when you're not.

Ventilation needn't be a major concern, but it's advisable to have a good supply of fresh air coming into the room while you exercise. Since you'll be taking in more air as your body works, the room can get stuffy quickly. Crack a window if there is one, or consider installing a ventilation fan. Exercise physiologists say a temperature of 70 to 72 degrees is ideal for exercising. If it's warmer,

you'll overheat more quickly—much colder and you could stiffen up.

Exercise offers lots of stimulation for your body, but sometimes not enough for your mind. Without something to occupy your mind, boredom can set in rather quickly. I consider some kind of entertainment system as important to a complete gym as the fitness equipment. A good stereo, or at least a set of extension speakers, will go a long way toward making an exercise room pleasant. If you can have a little fun while you work, the battle's half won.

Watching television is another option, although it's a little tough to do while you're lifting weights. Some home-gym owners like to give themselves a treat while exercising, like watching *The Love Boat* or tuning in some other program they'd feel too guilty to watch otherwise. Some friends of mine installed a big-screen set and video system in their home gym to make their sweat sessions more fun.

If you don't have a partner to work out with and don't like exercising alone, invite friends over to share your equipment. Make it a standing date for three or four evenings a week. And don't be surprised if before long some good-natured competition gets started among you.

## A HEALTHY INVESTMENT

So how much is it going to cost you to equip a gym of your own? Probably not as much as you think. There's nothing wrong with building your gym one piece at a time. Most people start with a stationary bike and add more aerobic equipment or a weight machine later on. The advantage to having different types of equipment is that it offers some variety and lessens the chance you'll get bored with the same routine every day.

As you'll see later on, you can spend $5,000 on a chrome-plated circuit trainer that will do just about everything for you but tie your shoes. But you can also pick up a perfectly decent weight machine for less than $700. And if that's still too steep, a good set of barbells only costs around $100.

I'd say most of the home gyms I've seen have about $1,000 to $2,000 worth of equipment in them. Sure you could buy a home computer for that, but it wouldn't help you to be healthier and live longer. And no matter how you programmed it, no computer could make you look as good as you want, but a well thought-out program in your home gym can.

# 2

# FEELING GOOD

Exercise is about realizing your full potential. It's about feeling and looking as good as you know you can. It means being leaner and trimmer, and having the energy to excel at work and at play. Exercise is pushing your limits and finding stores of strength and vigor you weren't sure existed.

Not all of us are living up to our potential. Two-thirds of Americans now work at sedentary jobs. In the Perrier/Harris poll mentioned in the last chapter, 50 percent of the people questioned said they felt they weren't getting enough exercise. Now how do you suppose they knew that? Undoubtedly it was because they looked in the mirror every morning and saw sallow skin and flab staring back at them, and because they didn't feel right. It's a funny thing, but your body will tell you when you're neglecting it. The message usually comes by way of a bad back, a steadily inflating spare tire, or a general feeling of lethargy. You feel as if you're lugging around an invisible ball and chain.

Now let's hear from the people in that same poll who work out regularly and know that they get enough exercise. When asked about the benefits of getting fit, 80 percent of them said it made them feel better in general. After that, they listed psychological benefits, feeling less tension, sleeping better, feeling more relaxed, looking better, and developing more self-discipline and a better self-image. In summing up the results, the Harris pollsters noted ". . . the more people are committed to regular exercise and physical exertion, the more they feel at one with themselves."

Perhaps the Harris folks were too decorous to ask, but a lot of people I know report that exercise has also improved their sex lives. "I never used to have the energy for sex, especially during the week," says a 38-year-old buddy of mine. "But since I started exercising [he puts in 20 minutes on his stationary bike after work every day and runs 9 miles a week] the old get-up-and-go came back. My wife's so happy about it, she wants to buy me a Soloflex machine for my birthday."

Working out hasn't released any dormant sex hormone in my friend. But he feels (and looks) better than he has in a long time. He's sexier to himself, and to others. Even his wardrobe has changed. Most importantly, he's improved his energy and stamina, two crucial ingredients of a great sex life.

But if you listen to enough born-again exercisers raving about their new lives, you might begin to suspect that some mass delusion is at work here. Fortunately, the scientific community has been listening, too, and has come to the rescue with some concrete evidence that getting and staying fit is good for you in a lot of ways. Here's a rundown on some of the areas they've explored, and what they found:

▶ *Skin*—This is a big one for those of us on the high side of 30. As we get older, our skin tends to get thin and stiffer, and eventually wrinkles form. In addition to releasing more sweat from glands, exercising opens up thousands of new capillaries in the skin, which bring more blood, oxygen and nutrients. In a University of California study, women who exercised regularly were found to have fewer wrinkles and better skin color than women in another group that didn't exercise. A similar study of male athletes in Finland showed that their skin was denser, thicker, stronger and more elastic than that of sedentary men.

▶ *Anxiety*—In a University of Southern California study, exercise was found to reduce neuromuscular activity and have a "significant tranquilizing effect." It produced both an immediate and a long-term reduction in anxiety after moderate levels of exercise. It's thought that working out may reduce the production of some stress hormones in the body. It's known that exercise releases more of your brain's endorphins, natural morphine-like compounds that reduce pain perception and leave you with a pleasant, calm feeling. And unlike prescription tranquilizers, endorphins have no known side effects.

▶ *Back pain*—Exercise and good posture can strengthen the back muscles and relieve pain. Doctors at New York Hospital now prescribe daily fitness training for patients with chronic back trouble. They report long-term positive results in 80 percent of the cases.

▶ *Migraines*—As anyone who has ever suffered from one of these blindingly painful head-aches may already know medication sometimes offers little or no relief. In some cases, the best advice doctors can offer sufferers of migraines, the causes of which aren't fully understood, is to lie in a dark, quiet room until the agony ends. But now there's a study from the University of Wisconsin which shows that an aerobic exercise program, performed in three 30-minute sessions a week, can reduce the frequency of migraines by half after 10 weeks. The doctors say that exercise may alter brain chemistry in some way, or perhaps it inhibits blood thickening, which can lead to headaches.

▶ *Digestion*—Exercise can help you get more from what you eat every day without any weight gain. Research at the University of California's Department of Nutritional Sciences found that riding a stationary bike for one hour a day helped subjects use the proteins and nutrients from their food more effectively.

▶ *Cholesterol*—You hear a lot of bad things about cholesterol, with good reason. High cholesterol levels in the blood have been linked with heart disease and the formation of gallstones. Cutting down on saturated animal fats is a key to controlling cholesterol and, apparently, so is exercise. Doctors working at the University of Cincinnati Medical Center discovered that patients who worked out for 10 to 20 minutes, three times weekly, excreted more cholesterol and lowered the levels of the substance in their blood.

▶ *Reaction time*—Common wisdom says you slow down as you get older. Not necessarily so, at least not if you stay fit. At San Diego State University, a group of subjects was asked to respond to the flashing of two lights by pressing a switch with the left or right index finger. The results showed that in sedentary individuals, the reaction time was longer the older the person was. But among the group that exercised regularly, there was little or no difference in reaction time, no matter what their age.

▶ *Diabetes*—Diabetes has now become our country's No. 3 killer. One of the prime factors, and one that exercise can help, is obesity. Your chances of having diabetes double for every 20 pounds you are overweight. But staying active may help in another way: by lowering blood sugar. At Yale University, testers found that when men worked out on a stationary bicycle four hours a week, the blood sugar taken up by their bodies' natural stores of insulin increased by 30 percent, lowering the overall levels.

▶ *Longevity*—In addition to making you feel better every day, fitness can help you have more days to feel good. One study of a group of laboratory rats showed that the female animals that exercised lived 11.5 percent longer, and the males 19.3 percent longer, than a corresponding group that did not exercise. If you're thinking "I'm not a rat," consider this sobering human statistic: The death rate among sedentary men aged 60 to 64 is five times higher than among men the same age who exercise.

Even if you feel good and the doctor just gave you a pat on the back, exercise can make you feel even better and stronger. It can give you more energy, strength, coordination, flexibility and endurance. You can become more effective at your work and play. And it can make you look better, too.

Why this pep talk? Because motivation is the most important element of any exercise program.

You've got to believe in the benefits because a real exercise program takes discipline and some work.

One of the best ways to get your daily workout into gear and to keep you going throughout it, is to fantasize about the benefits you're getting. If you exercise to lose weight, conjure a mental picture of your ideal body, lean and trim, as you pump away on that stationary bike.

When you're shopping for equipment, try to keep in mind not only what each piece will do for you, but how much you'll enjoy using it. And try to get as much of a variety as you can afford. Boredom is a serious enemy of any exercise program, and the best way to stave it off is by varying your daily routine as much as you can without deviating from your original program.

And finally, don't let your mind run ahead of your body. If you expect too much, too soon, you'll only be disappointed. Getting fit takes a little time. You may not see the benefits immediately, but don't get discouraged. There's no

one who won't respond and become healthier by exercising. Everyone differs in his or her rate of response. There are lots of reasons for that, among them age, general health, diet, stress, weight and body type. Keep at it and the payoff will eventually come.

Despite what some manufacturers might have you believe, there isn't any single, magic piece of equipment that gets your entire body into shape. You're made up of individual parts, most of which work in different ways. You've got to attack each body section differently. For example, hoisting barbells will make your arms and upper body stronger, but it won't do a thing for your legs, and very little for your heart and lungs. Running every day on a treadmill is great for your legs and cardiovascular system, but your upper body won't show a whole lot of gain. When designing your home gym, think about all the parts of your body and put together a selection of equipment that will help you get your *entire* body in shape.

In very general terms, there are two basic types of exercise: *aerobic* and *anaerobic*. The word aerobic literally means "with oxygen." This type of exercise gives your cardiovascular system a workout. It helps your heart pump more blood with each beat, which means it can beat more slowly and rest between beats. That means less stress on the heart and a decreased risk of heart attack. Aerobic exercise also improves the efficiency of your breathing. It increases the amount of air you take into your lungs with each breath. Aerobic exercise also trains your system to use the oxygen in your blood better to feed your muscles and organs, and it helps your body rid itself of carbon dioxide more effectively.

If you can choose only one type of exercise, aerobics are probably the best for overall health. Aerobic exercises are ones that really get you moving and pumping up your system. They include running, biking, rowing, calisthenics, jumping rope, and sports like tennis and racquetball.

Aerobic exercises get you huffing and puffing. They create a demand for oxygen, but with training, your body can supply it, and you can go on exercising for a long period. Anaerobic exercises, however, demand a great deal of oxygen in a very short time. Your body, no matter how well trained, can't provide all that's needed, so an oxygen debt occurs and you've got to stop for a while. Anaerobic activities like weight lifting and gymnastics can improve your speed, strength, balance and agility, as well as tone up your flabby spots.

For the most part, your body does what you ask it to do. If you sit around most nights watching TV, your muscles will deteriorate. Your heart and lungs will have to work harder to keep you going, since you don't seem interested in helping them. None of this is good for you, but you can't blame your body. Your muscles and cardiovascular system may be capable of doing twice as much for you, if only you'd ask.

Exercising sends a message to your body that more is going to be required of it. It responds by getting fitter, so that the next time you ask it will be better prepared.

Your body's response to the physical challenges you give it is known as the *training effect.* It revolves around the principle of overload. Your system will react by becoming fitter only if you ask it to do more than it normally does. If, for example, your arm muscles are adapted to regularly lifting 50-pound weights, you won't become any stronger unless you gradually increase that weight. Or if you do a lot of walking, you may need to run to benefit from a training effect.

If you are already reasonably fit when you start an exercise program, the training effect may be slow and almost unnoticeable at first. If you're an inactive person, the effect may be dramatic. In either case, your progress will eventually level off as you reach your potential. Potential varies from person to person, and a lot depends on things beyond your control such as age, height, heredity and body type.

To better understand what's taking place as you train, it may help to get to know your body and how it works a little better. The first thing to understand is how important oxygen is to your body. If the food you eat every day is the fuel you need for energy, oxygen is the flame you need to get it burning. Your body can lay in a good store of fuel, mostly in the form of fat, but it can't save up oxygen for a rainy day. Without a constant supply coming in, you won't stay alive for very long.

The system works this way: Your lungs take in oxygen from the air you breathe and pass it on to your blood. Your heart pumps the blood to your organs and muscles, where it's used to metabolize carbohydrates and fats— the food they need for energy. That's all well and good—until you want a little something extra. Say you're running to catch a

bus. Your muscles need some extra fuel to get those arms and legs moving, so your heart beats faster and you breathe more deeply, trying to supply the extra oxygen. If you catch the bus right away, your heart, lungs and muscles quickly recover and go back to their normal rhythms. But if the bus gets away and you've got to run a little further, an untrained system may not be able to keep up. The muscles will demand more oxygen than you can supply, and you'll have to stop.

The same things happen when you exercise. At first your system isn't equipped to handle the extra demands, and you'll tire quickly. Only as you adapt through the training effect will your capacity for exercise increase.

Perhaps the most dramatic physiological changes from exercise take place in the heart. When you first start a workout, no matter what your condition, the heart beats faster and the amount of blood it pumps with each beat— known as its *stroke volume*—increases. Your

blood also becomes more potent as the number of red corpuscles, which carry oxygen, increases. Finally, your blood vessels and capillaries open up further to accommodate the extra blood flowing into them.

The long-term effects of exercise on the heart are less immediate, but equally important. Like any other muscle, your heart gets larger and stronger the more it's used. With exercise, its stroke volume permanently increases, so that even when you're relaxing, your heart is pumping more blood than it used to with every beat. And that means it has to beat less and can rest longer between strokes. The size and flexibility of your veins and capillaries will also improve over the long term, offering less resistance to the flow of blood and making it still easier on your heart.

Keeping track of your heart rate, the number of times your heart beats in a minute, is an excellent way to monitor your fitness program. You should see a steady decrease over time as your heart becomes conditioned. To measure your resting pulse, you should take it in the morning just before getting out of bed. You can use one of the electronic meters described later in this book, or do it yourself. Place the first and second fingers of either hand (don't use your thumb as it will throw off the count) on the radial artery of the opposite wrist. The artery is located in the middle of your wrist, just below the base of the thumb. Wait a few seconds and then count the number of pulses for 10 seconds, counting the first beat as zero. Multiply that number by six for your heart rate per minute.

The average range for a man's heart rate is 68 to 80 beats per minute. A woman's is usually slightly higher, ranging from 75 to 85 beats per minute. Average doesn't mean ideal, since it includes all those people who don't get much exercise. In fact, a fit heart may beat 30 percent fewer times in a minute. A fellow I know once alarmed his family doctor at a check-up with a heart rate of 34 beats per minute. The

doctor ordered an immediate set of EKG tests, which only showed that my friend's weight lifting, half-hour daily workouts on a stationary bike and 10-mile jogs twice a week had made his heart so efficient it could beat half as often as an average man's. You may not want to aim quite that low, but consider that if your heart rate is now average and you can knock off 25 percent, you'll be saving your poor overworked heart several million beats in the course of a year!

Keeping a daily heart-rate log will help you see what exercise is doing for you. Don't be dismayed if your rate is lower one day and slightly higher the next. Fluctuations are normal, but in a few weeks your chart should show an overall downward progression.

Your lungs will also reap long-term benefits from exercising. At first they may have a hard time keeping up with you as you work out. If your lungs are unused to deep breathing, they won't be able to meet the oxygen demands you're

putting on them for very long. But that will change. The thing to remember is that your lungs have no muscles. They don't initiate the in-and-out action of breathing. That job is done by the muscles in your chest and abdomen. Those muscles can get lazy from years of shallow breathing, but as you get fitter they'll get stronger. The result will be that you breathe more deeply and fill your lungs more completely, even when you're not exercising.

Changes take place inside the lungs as well. As you breathe more deeply, you bring into play more of the lung's alveoli, the air sacs that transfer oxygen to the blood. Exercising also opens up more new capillaries, further streamlining oxygen exchange. As a result, when a trained person takes a breath, his or her lung tissues may be extracting 300 percent more oxygen from the air than an unfit person. The result of more efficient breathing is similar to what happens to your heart, you breathe less to get the oxygen you need. If you're not in shape, you may be taking a breath once a second. After an exercise program, you can halve that number.

Toning up your muscles, and that doesn't necessarily mean building a physique to Arnold Schwarzenegger proportions, can also make your body a more efficient machine. Lifting even light weights, using one of the many resistance multi-gyms, or pumping your arms and legs up on a rowing machine or stationary bike will firm up your muscles and streamline your body, as well as make you more limber, agile, graceful, coordinated and stronger.

When you put muscles through their paces, they immediately respond by calling for extra blood supply. Long disused capillaries fill up with blood and the muscle becomes larger and warmer. As they heat up, the muscles become less stiff and more pliable. After the workout they are much more relaxed than before, which is what gives you that laid-back feeling after a good sweat session. (Tranquilizers like Valium, after all, are really only muscle relaxants.) The pumping of muscles during a workout, especially an aerobic one like bicycling, running or rowing, squeezes the veins together which helps to push the blood out, relieving some of the workload on the heart.

Over time, exercise also has permanent benefits. The medical jury is still out on whether new muscle fibers are created, but it is known that exercise strengthens and thickens existing fibers, which makes the muscles harder and sometimes larger. What's happening, say the experts, is that using muscles stimulates a protein which makes them stronger. But for that to happen, you've got to eat a balanced diet and exercise as well to give the muscles the nutrients they need to make more of the proteins.

Women needn't worry about sprouting sleeve-busting biceps. It just isn't possible, no matter how much weight they lift or how often they do it. The large muscle bulk that some males develop as a result of lifting weights is because of the male hormone testosterone. Before they reach puberty, girls and boys have muscles that are about the same in size and strength. But at puberty, testosterone is released from the male's testes and estrogen from the female's ovaries. These hormones bring out the sexual characteristics, and things begin to change. With about 100 times more testosterone in their systems than women, males develop larger muscles and more muscle tissue—about 10 percent more than women.

Except for a tiny percentage of women who have inherited large muscles or larger than normal levels of testosterone, there's little chance of adding more than a fraction of an inch to any muscle's circumference if you're female. But there's no difference in levels of muscle endurance between the sexes, and women still get all the other benefits of weight lifting, even if in a trimmer package.

As with the cardiovascular system, gains in muscular fitness come only if the muscles are overloaded. The way to overload muscles is to pit them against some kind of resistance, and increase that resistance gradually as the muscles adapt. There are two different ways to apply resistance to muscles: isometric and isotonic.

*Isometric* exercises force a muscle to contract without any movement; the muscle is in a fixed position when it meets the resistance. Some examples of isometric exercises are pushing against a wall, clenching a fist or pushing one hand against the other.

One good thing that can be said about isometric exercise is that it's cheap. You don't need any equipment, and you can do it while waiting in the check-out line. But there are certainly better ways to give your muscles some attention. Since the resistance isn't applied through any range of motions, isometrics offer very limited gains. If you spend 20 minutes a day pressing against a wall as hard as you can, you will end up with more power, *but only when your arms are in that position.*

Isometrics do build muscle bulk, but it's the "muscle-bound" type that isn't of much use. And isometrics do nothing for cardiovascular fitness.

*Isotonic* means "with weights," and this type of exercise offers conditioning over a much wider range of movements. With weights, resistance is applied through both the contraction and extension of a muscle.

Free weights, such as barbells and dumbbells, are the cheapest type of equipment for isotonic training. By themselves, though, they limit you to working on your upper body and arms. But by adding various accessories like squat racks, leg extension and curl benches or pull-down mechanisms, you can use weights to work on just about all the major muscle groups. Many companies now make multi-gyms that combine a number of these accessories in one unit. You buy one set of weights and switch them from station to station as you need them.

The main shortcoming of using weights this way is

that the resistance of a muscle or group of muscles varies greatly throughout the movement of a lift. Thanks to the natural leverage system of arms and legs, the lift becomes "easier" once you've overcome the initial resistance. In other words, once you've gotten it off the ground, you've done the hardest part. Of course, you'll get some benefit through the range of motions, but not as much as in the beginning. And if, for example, you're lifting weights to train for a sport like tennis, you may need strength through the full range for a mean backhand.

Variable-resistance weight machines were developed to overcome the problem. They use pulleys with flat, stacked weights to provide equal amounts of resistance through all parts of exercise movements. And whereas barbells are lifted with explosive, jerky movements that can lead to muscle and tendon injuries, the pulleys in variable-resistance machines tend to smooth out the lifting action.

A refinement of variable-resistance equipment is the Nautilus system. In addition to weights and pulleys Nautilus equipment uses an aluminum cam to create a rotary movement, similar to the natural movement of your joints when they're in motion. This makes the equipment particularly useful for sports training.

Finally, no discussion of the benefits of exercise would be complete without mentioning the positive effect of exercise on the skeleton, that structure that holds together all those muscles you work on. Asked to list the reasons for working out, the first thing out of most people's mouths isn't likely to be, "To build up my skeletal system." But think of it as a hidden benefit.

As people get older, their bones lose calcium and become thinner and more brittle. Age-related bone loss affects about six million men and women in this country alone. As many as 350,000 of the one million broken bones suffered by women over 45 every year in the U.S. can be traced to this bone loss,

known as osteoporosis.

Osteoporosis is often linked to the aging process itself, but now there's evidence that the real cause may be that as people age they become less active. In one test it was found that women with an average age of 53 who exercised for one hour three times a week actually *gained* 2.6 percent in bone mass over the course of a year.

What seems to be happening is that the added stress put on bones from exercise, combined with the improved blood supply, causes them to increase in strength and thickness. It may not make you look better in a bikini, but it might insure that you'll still be swimming when you're 65.

But what about that bikini? Weight loss is a reason people often *do* give for exercising. And they're on the right track, because staying fit is an important part of getting and staying thin.

High-carbohydrate, low-fat, high-fat, low-carbohydrate—all the fad diets have one thing in common: They're too

concerned with the number of calories going in, and not concerned enough with how many are going out. Just as dieting will reduce the number of calories you get each day, exercise will increase the number that you burn up. You can atone for a binge of a big slice of chocolate cake by starving yourself the next day, or by jumping on your stationary bike and pedaling for half-an-hour.

Better yet, skip the cake and still do the 30 minutes of exercise. The best way to lose weight is to cut down moderately on the calories you eat while treating yourself to regular workouts. If you've tried dieting without the exercise and were disappointed, there may be a good reason. Studies have shown that with diet alone, most people lose more muscle tissue than fat. In some cases, the weight loss was 70 percent muscle and 30 percent fat.

Losing all that muscle isn't good for you, and it's likely to leave you feeling run down and weak. That will give you as good an excuse as any to quit dieting. But by putting exercise on your diet menu, the ratio of fat to muscle lost will be reversed and you'll end up with more energy, not less.

When you first start the day's exercise, you may be burning mostly carbohydrates for muscle fuel, with just a tiny bit of fat thrown into the fire. But keep at it and in only 20 minutes, you'll be igniting half carbohydrates and half fat. Keep at it and the percentage of fat you burn will continue to increase.

And there's better news still. It seems that once you've "trained" your system to burn fat, if you stay fit you can continue to burn it up *even when you're not exercising.* Tests have proven that your metabolism, once it's speeded up, can stay that way for 24 hours or more. So even while you sleep, your revved-up body will be consuming those calories.

If you have to choose either dieting or exercise for weight control, exercise may be the better bet. If you continue to eat the same amount of food but work out regularly, you should lose pounds. The odds are, you'll probably find yourself eating less anyway because exercise is known to suppress the appetite. The reasons why exercisers eat less aren't absolutely clear, but one theory is that since a lower body temperature is one signal to the brain that it's chow time, and exercise raises your temperature, you're fooling yourself into thinking you're not hungry. It could also be that the higher levels of certain body chemicals in the blood after exercise, particularly adrenaline, may inhibit your urge to eat. Whatever the reasons, the next time you feel the urge to launch a midnight assault on the refrigerator, consider attacking your fitness equipment instead.

With all this good news about exercise, you might be wondering when the bad news is coming. The truth is, there doesn't seem to be much. Scour the reams of research, studies and reports published every year on physical fitness and you'll be hard pressed to find many that say exercise is bad for you. No matter what your present condition or health, some type of extra activity can make you feel and look better.

# 3

# THE WORKOUT

Since there aren't too many rules about when to exercise, now is as good a time as any. Do it when it feels right and when it's most convenient for *you*. The great thing about having your own gym at home is that you don't have to fit your workouts into anyone else's hours. When the mood strikes you, head for the equipment. Vary the times that you exercise if you want. It will keep the routine from becoming boring or predictable.

Some people like to start their juices flowing early by exercising in the morning. It makes them feel better all day and they've accomplished something, even if things don't go too well at the office. If you choose mornings as your training time, just remember that your muscles and joints are stiffer the earlier in the day it is, so warming up may take a bit longer.

The lunch hour is also a great time for a workout. It breaks up the day, gives you an energy lift, and is a whole lot healthier than a three-martini meal. Later on I'll tell you about some portable fitness equipment that fits in a briefcase, so you can take your gym to the office with you.

Use an evening session to unwind from a long day and to ease away the tensions of work. You can pedal six miles on a stationary bike in the time it takes Dan Rather to fill you in on the events of the day. Exercise is an effective way to cut your appetite at dinner, but if you've already eaten, wait a couple of hours before going at it. Exercise and digestion both demand a lot of blood—in different places—and it's best to let them each have it without interference from the other.

If a session later in the evening is more to your liking, that's fine, too. Just give yourself an hour before going to bed to allow your adrenaline level time to drop back to normal.

And just one more rule: If you drink, don't drive . . . and don't exercise either. Your coordination will be way off, and alcohol constricts blood vessels and interferes with oxygen transfer.

No matter what time you schedule your workout, allow at least 10, and preferably 20 minutes beforehand, to warm yourself up. Your car won't run very well before it's warmed up and neither will your body. You need to move around and stretch before you will be ready for more strenuous work.

A warm-up should get you warmed up, not all hot and bothered. The goal is to

get your lungs bringing in more oxygen and your heart pumping faster, to get your body prepared for action. You should work hard enough to perspire a little, but not so strenuously that you're soaking with sweat.

The main reason for warming up is to prevent injuries. Catapulting a resting heart into vigorous exercise can catch it unawares and cause it to beat irregularly. Cold, tight muscles are much more likely to tear than warm, flexible ones. And joints that are rusty from inactivity can cause you serious pain after a workout, unless they are gently put through a full range of motions beforehand.

A round of preliminary exercises will raise your body temperature and pump extra blood into your muscles, waking up snoozing blood vessels. It will make them more relaxed but at the same time stronger.

Don't skimp on your warm-up period. You may save a little time by cutting it short, but you could

throw your whole exercise program off schedule with an injury.

Start the warm-up by walking briskly around your gym area 10 or 15 times, pumping your arms or swinging them back in forth in front of you. If your area is too small to make a circuit practical, just jog in place for 5 minutes.

Next move on to some calisthenics. I know, they bring back bad memories of smelly junior-high gyms. Only now, you're not doing calisthenics because some crabby teacher told you to, you're doing them because they're good for you. Doing calisthenics to music with a strong beat should make them more fun than they used to be.

Just in case you've blotted them from your mind, here's a refresher course: Calisthenics 101:

▶ *Jumping jacks:* Begin with your feet together and hands at your sides. Now jump, spreading your legs to about shoulder width while at the same time bringing your arms up until you can touch your hands directly over your head. Return to the beginning position. Do 30 of these if you can.

▶ *Push-ups:* The right way to do a push-up is to stretch out on the floor with your arms at shoulder width and your legs and lower body supported by your bent toes. Now slowly lower yourself until your face almost touches the floor, then push back up again. Make sure that your legs and back stay straight throughout the exercise. Try to do 10 or 15 repetitions.

If regular push-ups are too hard at first, try them with your knees touching the floor. Soon you'll find you're ready for the straight-leg kind.

▶ *Sit-ups:* While they warm you up, sit-ups also help tighten back and stomach muscles. Lay on your back on the floor with your arms extended straight up past your head. Slowly and smoothly propel yourself into a sitting position, bringing your arms slowly up and over to touch your knees with your hands. For this type of sit-up it's important to keep your feet on the floor at all times for maximum benefit. Ask someone to hold your ankles down, or look into one of the straps or bars designed for sit-ups that are mentioned in the equipment section of this book.

An easier version of the sit-up is done with the knees bent. With either kind, start with 10 if you're out of shape, and add another every day or two until you've worked your way up to 30.

▶ *Chin-ups:* A chin-up bar is a great addition to any home gym. Just make sure that wherever you install one, it's firmly anchored, since you'll be putting a lot of strain on it.

To do a chin-up, grasp the bar with your palms facing you and pull your body up until you can touch the bar with your chin. This exercise is tough, since you are lifting the equivalent of your own weight. There really isn't an easier version, so just do as many as you comfortably can.

▶ *Squats:* This exercise will start the blood pumping into your legs. Grip the top of a chair that's facing away from you, or a wall bar placed at about waist level and squat down into a sitting position. Stand up straight again and repeat. You ought to easily be able to do 30 of these after a week or so.

Continuing the warm-up, move on to some stretching exercises. Stretching is an absolutely vital part of any total fitness program. It loosens and relaxes the muscles and makes your whole body more flexible. The elasticity of muscles, tendons and ligaments can have a profound effect on your performance. Numerous studies have shown that flexible athletes are better athletes. Other surveys have proven that far fewer sports injuries occur when the activity is preceded by controlled stretching movements.

There are right and wrong ways to stretch your muscles. That junior-high gym teacher may have told you the best exercises for stretching involved bouncing up and down. Wrong! Ballistic, or bouncing exercises can do more harm than good. With rapid, bouncing movements, there's no way to control the stretch. You may force muscles to pull much farther than you should, but you'll only find out after it happens, when the pain comes. In ballistic movements, your muscles contract against the forceful stretch, creating much more tension than from a slow, easy movement. The result of that tension, sooner or later, will be torn muscle fibers.

Instead of bouncing and jerking muscles into submission, ease them into an extension gradually and gently. You'll be able to feel the stretch as it progresses, and you can stop immediately if there's any discomfort or strain.

Static stretching is the kind that gets the nod from most sports doctors these days. It involves stretching a muscle or group of muscles into position,

holding the position for a slow count to 10, then releasing. Each static exercise is usually repeated at least five times, but repetitions are alternated with other exercises.

According to Dr. John Bealieu in *The Physician and Sportsmedicine,* "Compared to other techniques, static stretching produces the least amount of tension and is the safest method of improving flexibility."

A list of some good static stretching movements follows. Repeat each exercise, but don't do the same one twice in a row. In other words, do one set of each stretch, then come back and start from the beginning. It will give each muscle a chance to recover and benefit.

▶ *Calves and ankles:* Sit on a chair or the edge of a weight bench with your legs straight out in front of you. Keep your heels together but turn the tips of your feet away from each other as far as you can and hold. Now move your heels apart about a foot and turn the tips of

your feet toward each other and hold again.

Another effective calf exercise is to sit on the floor with your legs straight out in front of you and try to move the tops of your feet as far back toward you as you can. Hold that position for 30 seconds and release. If you find it easier, wrap a towel around the balls of your feet, grasp an end in each hand and gently pull your toes toward you.

▶ *Waist:* Stand with your feet apart at shoulder width and your arms out. Gently twist your upper body clockwise, keeping your hips and legs stationary. Hold, return to your starting position and twist in the other direction.

▶ *Arms:* With your palm flat and elbow slightly bent, use one arm to reach for the sky, stretching it as far as you can. Hold. Now lower that arm and reach with the other.

▶ *Neck:* Sit on a bench or a mat on the floor. Start with your head pointing straight forward and your chin up. Turn your head to the right until you can feel your neck muscles stretching. Hold, return to your original position then turn your head to the left and hold. Straighten your head, then try to touch your right ear to your right shoulder. If you can't make it all the way, go as far as you can and hold. Return, and do the same thing with the other side. Now looking straight ahead, point your chin toward the ceiling, hold, then point it toward your chest and hold again.

A round of the recommended calisthenics and stretching exercises should have gotten most of your joints into the act. Just to be on the safe side though, go through some bending and rotating motions with your wrists, elbows, shoulders, hips, knees and ankles. Those creaks and cracks will tell you which areas have been neglected.

Although these warm-up routines were designed to shift you into gear for a more strenuous session, you might want to get in the habit of doing them daily. They'll help keep you limber and frisky all day, especially if you do them first thing in the morning.

As far as your actual workout goes, you don't have to keep at it every day. In fact, you probably shouldn't. While your body can recover from light exercise in a matter of hours, it usually takes a full day or more to recuperate from strenuous activity.

For most people three sessions a week, lasting 20 to 30 minutes each, are adequate. More weekly workouts generally won't get you any more fit nor will they get you in shape much more quickly, so it's a matter of diminishing returns. But fewer sessions aren't a good idea either, since skipping exercise for more than 48 straight hours allows your body to start *de*conditioning which means you'll lose ground. I like to get my hard exercise sessions in on Monday, Wednesday and Friday, and then get outdoors for some activity like tennis, jogging or a brisk walk on the weekend.

▶ *TRAINING RINGS*

*Model 423*

LECO INTERNATIONAL
48 BURD ST.
NYACK, NY 10960
(914) 358-7770

PRICE: $20

You can make like an Olympic gymnast with a set of these training rings in your gym. They're great for warming up. This brand has molded plastic handles and woven nylon webbing. Of course, if you don't live in a loft you'll probably need to hang them in the attic or some other room with a very high ceiling.

The goals you set for yourself will determine the pace of your regular workouts. Ideally, you'll want to strive for total body fitness—stronger and more efficient heart, lungs and muscles. How quickly you arrive at that stage is entirely up to you. It's much better to go easy at first and methodically build a healthier body. There's far less chance that you'll strain yourself or cause an injury if you progress one step at a time.

Be realistic. If you're a desk jockey who gets winded climbing a couple of flights of stairs, don't promise yourself you'll ride 20 minutes straight on your exercise bike the first day. Chances are that in less than half that time your heart will be pounding like a jackhammer, and you'll hop off disappointed in yourself.

You've got to walk before you can run. A better way to approach aerobic exercise like stationary biking, rowing or using a treadmill is to start with a 5-minute session and keep it up until you can do it easily. (Usually that will only take about a week.) Then increase your workout time in 5-minute increments until you can do 20 minutes without gasping.

If you're using equipment with adjustable resistance—and you should—the next step is to do the 20 minutes at a higher setting, gradually increasing the amount of resistance you are working against over several weeks.

One target to consider for aerobic workouts is to push your heart rate up to 70 or 80 percent of maximum and keep it there for 20 or 30 minutes. The maximum possible heart rate for humans is about 220 beats per minute, but as you get older, your maximum decreases by approximately one beat per minute a year. To calculate your present maximum rate, subtract your age from 220.

If you're younger than 35, aim for a workout that keeps you at 80 percent of your maximum. If you're over 35, a goal of 70 percent is safer.

As I mentioned earlier, there are electronic pulse meters that can be worn while you exercise, and some stationary bikes come with pulse sensors built into the handlebars. Either type will help you monitor your pulse constantly. If you don't have a pulse meter, just stop once or twice during your exercise session, take your pulse by hand for 10 seconds and multiply by six.

Even if you can't maintain your optimum percentage for the entire 20 or 30 minutes right away, it's a worthy objective. Tests show that numerous short bouts of ''high-heart-rate'' exercise with rests in between aren't as beneficial as one long session where the heart rate is maintained for the entire time.

The benefits of aerobic exercise are general. It works simultaneously on the heart, lungs and circulatory system. There's no real way to isolate any cardiovascular function for special attention. But with weight training you can choose the part or parts of your body that need strengthening and shaping and concentrate only on them if you like. There are specific pieces of both free weight and variable resistance equipment designed for every major muscle group, and some minor ones, too. Circuit trainers, like those made by Nautilus and Universal, combine five or six of the most popular weight-training devices in one unit.

As well as being able to pick which muscles you want to work on, you also have a choice on how you want to work on them. High-resistance, low-repetition exercises build muscle bulk and, to some degree, strength. Low-resistance, high-repetition exercises are better for muscular endurance, weight loss and for streamlining your body.

High resistance, low repetition simply means lifting a lot of weight a few times. It's how many of the men you see in the muscle magazines get those enormous pectorals. If you long to boast that you can bench press 220 pounds, or want bullies to quit kicking sand in your face, this is the training method for you. Otherwise, it has its limitations. For one thing, very few activities in life require only strength. Endurance, agility, coordination and speed are usually equally important, and high-resistance

exercise offers none of those things. In some sports, such as tennis, racquetball and golf, bulky upper-body muscles may actually be a hindrance. There's also a risk of taking the training too far and winding up with muscles so large they interfere with each other and leave you muscle-bound.

If you really want to go this route, go easy at first! According to Marijeanne Liederbach of the Institute of Sports Medicine at New York's Lenox Hill Hospital, weight lifting injuries generally happen when people try to hoist too much too soon. "It's very important to start slowly," she cautions. "It's also essential that the posture and bone alignment be right. I'd suggest that anyone thinking about weight training talk to a professional trainer first to get the basics."

A series of low-resistance, high-repetition exercises will result in more well-rounded fitness, or I should say more well-proportioned fitness. Lifting small amounts of weight numerous times won't give

you huge muscles, but will still give you muscle definition for a trimmer look. In addition, it provides a lot of things that heavy weight training doesn't, like endurance and flexibility.

Don't be ashamed to begin with as little as 5 pounds of weight. The thing here is how many times, not how much, you lift. A good start is to see if you can lift the 5 pounds 10 or 15 times. If you can, it's time to add more weight, 5 pounds at a time. Once you can lift that 15 times without stopping, add more. But any time you can't do at least eight repetitions, go back to a lighter load and work up slowly.

For each body area you are trying to improve, do three groups of repetitions, or sets, at each workout. Alternate the sets so that you do a full round on each muscle group before you start over again on the second set. That way, the muscles will have the few minutes they need to recover between sets.

Never get so involved in your exercise that you

## EXERCISE AND YOUR DOCTOR

How healthy do you have to be before you can exercise to get healthier? A lot of fitness books and television shows post a big, bold-faced warning right at the beginning cautioning everyone to run to their doctors before attempting push-up No. 1. It's enough to scare you into staying on the couch.

In truth, there's no unanimous agreement, even within the medical community, on who should see a doctor and when. The American Heart Association takes a conservative stance: Visit your doctor before starting an exercise program. But Kenneth H. Cooper, M.D., author of *Aerobics* and numerous other fitness books, doesn't think that's always necessary. He says that before getting serious about exercise you should:

· Have seen a doctor within the past year if you're under 30.
· Have seen a doctor within the past six months if you're 30-35.
· Have seen a doctor in the past three months if you're over 35.

To that I'd add: See a doctor if you have a history of heart trouble, are obese or a heavy smoker (20 or more cigarettes a day), or suffer from arthritis. And stop exercising immediately if you experience an abnormal heartbeat, pain in your chest, dizziness, light-headedness or fainting. Consult a physician before starting up your program again.

Even if the doctor finds a problem, it doesn't necessarily mean you won't be able to exercise at all. You'll just have to take it a little more slow and easy, or work out in a prescribed program.

One thing seems a sure bet. Moderate exercise is less of a risk than no exercise at all.

forget to breathe. That may sound a bit silly, but it happens often enough for doctors to have given the result a name: the *Valsalva effect.* What happens is that when you hold your breath during muscle contractions, your throat constricts and blood return to the heart decreases and your blood pressure drops. Just when you need oxygen the most it's not available, and the effects are dizziness, headache and even blackout.

Instead of holding your breath, try to exhale with each muscle contraction. In other words, breathe *out* when you lift the weight and *in* when you bring it down.

After an intense workout it's natural to want to sit or lay down for a few minutes to enjoy the post-exercise glow. But don't be too hasty. Switching abruptly from vigorous activity to rest can lead to problems. Cooling down for a few minutes after exercising is just as important as warming up beforehand.

As you exercise, your heart pumps blood down to your muscles to supply

oxygen for fuel. In return, the squeezing action of the muscles helps return the blood to the heart. If you stop suddenly your heart will still be pumping like mad, but your muscles won't be pitching in their help anymore. Getting the blood back can put an enormous strain on the heart and if you relax totally too soon, blood will pool in the extremities, depriving the brain of oxygen and causing dizziness.

When muscles are working and burning energy, they also generate wastes like lactic acid. If wastes aren't pumped away after exercise, the chemicals remain in the muscles and leave them sore. Keeping the heart and muscles pumping together for awhile will carry away the wastes to be harmlessly dispersed.

So before you take a rest, keep moving around for 5 minutes after your workout. You don't need to do any special exercises, just walk around flexing your arms and legs for awhile. If you've been using a stationary bike, rowing

## NO WORK, NO PAY

Sit back, relax, and leave the exercising to some gizmo. The offers certainly do sound enticing. You usually find them in the backs of magazines, along with the ads for miracle creams that will grow hair on Telly Savalas. Passive exercise devices, according to the claims, will shake, rattle, roll, massage, sweat and electrically stimulate you to a state of perfect fitness without your so much as flexing a muscle on your own.

Sorry folks, it sounds too easy to be true because it is. The unfortunate truth is, unless you tax your muscles, heart and lungs through *real* exercise—the kind that makes you *feel* like you've done some work—there's very little to be gained.

The whole passive thing probably got started by those motorized vibrating belts you used to see in all the gyms. The idea was to buckle yourself in, flip a switch, and the jiggling motion of the belt would slough off all your cellulite and tone up your muscles. In fact, there's absolutely no evidence that these machines do anything but perhaps relax you a bit. They make me feel seasick.

More recent gimmicks are the sauna suits and sauna pants, rubberized, metalic and sometimes inflatable clothes that make you look like an extra in a Grade Z 1950s science fiction movie. They're supposed to make you sweat off weight while you walk around the house. You'll sweat all right (you may overheat, too), but what miniscule poundage you might lose is strictly water. Drink a tall glass of lemonade later and you'll be your old self again.

But perhaps the most alluring of all the passive gadgets are the electronic muscle stimulators. Several companies make them, but the claims usually sound

machine or treadmill, simply taper off your speed gradually to give your system time to adjust. Then take the break you've earned.

Even with the best precautions, an occasional muscle soreness isn't out of the ordinary. If it's going to happen, it usually occurs 24 to 48 hours after a workout and lasts for a day or so. Doctors don't seem to know exactly why sore muscles follow some exercise sessions and not others, but they think it may be due to changes in the muscles' connective tissues. Anyway, it's nothing to worry about. When it happens, treat the area with hot packs or soak in a tub of warm water. Skip your next workout if you're still tender and substitute some easy exercise or stretching.

How long does it take to get fit? It's a common question, although there isn't a standard answer. A lot depends on how good or bad your condition was when you started, as well as your age and general health. Expect to make steady progress for 4 to 16 weeks, after which the

improvement may level off. That's the signal that you're approaching peak fitness and can switch to a maintenance program. It's the payoff. Now you can exercise just enough to maintain what you've gained. Decrease the intensity of each workout if you like, or cut down from three to two sessions a week. Whatever you do, don't rest on your laurels. If you lay off altogether, the fitness you've worked so hard to get will slip away at a rate of about 10 percent a week. In a few months you'll be back where you began.

That's about it for the basics of a general exercise program. But most of us have one or two areas that need special attention—a spare tire, a bad back or some other problem. Here's a rundown on some ways to concentrate on specific parts of your body:

## TUMMY TRIMMING

Did you ever look at a 10-year-old picture of yourself at the beach and marvel at what a flat alike: "3,000 sit-ups without moving an inch!" "Lie still and lose pounds."

These wonders are supposed to take place with the help of a small transformer with attached electrodes that are placed on various parts of the body. When the juice is turned on, low-voltage current twitches the muscles, and presumably gives them a workout while you lie back and enjoy the tingle.

Electronic muscle stimulators do have their uses, but none of them has anything to do with losing weight or getting fit. Physical therapists sometimes use special types to help bedridden patients prevent muscle atrophy and to relax muscle spasms. But again, there is no proof that they'll "turn paunch and love handles into muscle," or lighten anything but your wallet. Recently, the U.S. Food and Drug Administration ordered one company, Bio-Tone, to stop advertising their electronic stimulator as "effective for losing weight, reducing girth, or eliminating cellulite." Until someone comes up with a legitimate way to get fit without working, do it the old-fashioned way: *Earn* it.

### THE WELL-DRESSED ATHLETE

It used to be that a lumpy gray-fleece sweatsuit and a T-shirt stolen from gym class years ago were about as stylish as exercise togs got. The "functional chic" look is still popular among some athletes, mostly men, but exercise clothes have definitely come out of the locker and into the world of fashion.

Nowadays sweatsuits come in so many attractive cuts and colors that in some places they've replaced jeans as *de rigueur* casual wear outside the gym. Not long ago I saw a gorgeous woman

stomach you *used* to have? It may seem that growing up means growing out, too, but it doesn't have to be that way. You can look that good in a bathing suit again.

Exercise can help, but you'll have to give it a hand by watching those calories. Of course, there's no guarantee that dieting will take weight off any special area, but the stomach does seem to be one of the places that responds first.

As dieting takes off the flab, you can be tightening and defining your stomach muscles with exercise. Sit-ups are a good way to start. Once you can do 50 or 60, try using a slant board or incline bench. Keep adjusting the angle as your muscles adapt.

Working out with weights can flatten your stomach, too. One of the best movements is the *curl*—lifting the weight toward your chest with your elbows tucked in close at your sides. Concentrate on doing many repetitions, not lifting lots of pounds.

Leg weights that attach to your sneakers or wrap around your ankles with

Velcro closures are great for adding oomph to stomach-tightening calisthenics. After attaching them, try lying on your side and lifting the opposite leg high as many times as you can. Then switch sides.

Forget about belly belts or any type of clothing that promises a slimmer stomach. When they're on they hold you in, like a girdle would, but there's no lasting benefit.

## BREASTS

In spite of what a lot of advertisers would like you to believe, nothing short of implant surgery can actually increase breast size. I've seen everything from suction devices to hypnotism touted as breast developers, but it's all a lot of hot air. Breasts are mostly fat, glands and blood vessels. There's no muscle there, nothing to develop.

That's not to say you can't make the most of what you were born with. There are muscles underneath the breasts that lift and support them, and these muscles strolling up Rodeo Drive in Beverly Hills wearing a tailored sweatsuit and about $5,000 worth of gold jewelry.

Leotards have also matured from basic blue to a rainbow of colors and stripes, polka dots and geometric patterns. And the college T-shirt has given way to tops emblazoned with messages like "Body by Effort," "Weights Before Dates" and "Bodybuilding Gives Me a Lift."

You won't catch me with a bad word to say about sweat style. It makes perfect sense to look good while you're working out to look even better. But let me leave you with a few words of caution to remember the next time you're shopping for exercise outfits: Looks aren't everything. Sports clothes should protect you as well as project a statement about you, so keep these tips in mind when you're in the market for a new workout wardrobe:

• *Bras*—Even though it does undercover work, a sports bra is the single most important piece of protective clothing most women can buy. When female athletes at 115 colleges and universities in the United States were surveyed a few years ago, 72 percent said they experienced some breast soreness after exercise. The reason for the pain, undoubtedly, was that the women's bras weren't offering enough support.

When women exercise, particularly when it involves jumping or bouncing exercises like calisthenics or treadmill running, their breasts get quite a jiggling. It may look great on reruns of *Charlie's Angels,* but it's very bad for the breasts. The only thing that holds a breast's shape is the skin that surrounds it. A lot of unrestrained bouncing, along with aging, can lead to sagging. At the same time, breast movement strains

can be firmed and toned. It will make the most of what you've got.

The chest muscles (pectorals) respond to several kinds of weight lifting exercises. One is called a *fly* and it involves pulling weights from an arms-outstretched position across the chest. You can do flys with dumbbells or resistance weights on a pulley system attached to ropes and handles. Nautilus and other companies make special fly machines with padded arms that are used to pull resistance forward with your inner arms.

The *bench press* is another excellent chest-muscle builder and it, too, can be performed with free weights or machines. When you press a weight you actually are pushing it away from you. When pressing barbells you'll need to use a bench, since your elbows need to be bent at about 30 degrees in the starting position. That puts them below your back, a position that's just about impossible if you're working on the floor. To press barbells you simply start in that position with the bar at chest level

and push the weights above you until your elbows are straight. *Always* work with a spotter close by when bench pressing a lot of weight, since you may not be able to control the barbell as well as when you're doing high reps with relatively light weights.

An obvious advantage of using variable-resistance machines for presses is that you'll never need a spotter, since the weights will be behind you and are controlled by the pulley system.

## THIGHS

Let's clear something up right from the start: Cellulite is just a fancy French word for fat. Calling it by a foreign name just makes fat seem more mysterious and allows some unscrupulous entrepreneurs to market useless gadgets and creams to "melt" it away.

The thighs seem to be a place where flab feels at home. Heavy thighs are among the most common complaints women voice about their bodies. Once again, there's no way to the underlying muscles and causes soreness as well as further undermining support.

The larger your breasts, the more you need a special sports bra. Women who wear a D-cup are far more likely to report pain after exercise than those who wear an A-cup. Larger breasts weigh more and thus create more of a pull when they bounce.

A well-made sports bra will usually have a wide back with fasteners that are covered to prevent chafing. Straps should be nonelastic to reduce stretching. Look for one with cups made of cotton or cotton blend, and make sure that the seams are covered to avoid "jogger's nipple," a chafing ailment that also affects men who wear shirts with rough seams.

Before you buy a sports bra, try it on. Jump up and down a few times in the dressing room to test the bra. If your breasts bounce at all, keep shopping.

• *Jockstraps*—In my school, anyone who showed up for gym class without a jock on would get sent to the showers. In your home gym there's no vigilant coach checking up on you, so you're on your own. Most men don't need to be told that even a slight bump to the testicles can be awfully painful and potentially dangerous. A jockstrap is still the best way to avoid such problems. Cut the coach's picture out of an old yearbook and paste it to the wall of your changing room as a reminder if you have to, but don't forget to wear a jock.
• *Shoes*—Politics and religion aside, I can't think of another subject that causes more debate among my friends than which running or sports shoe is best. Someone is forever coming to me to extol the virtues of some

spot reduce, but an effective diet and exercise program will eventually take weight off your entire body, thighs included.

At the same time, doing exercises designed to tone thigh muscles will make your legs look tighter and leaner. Sometimes the "spread" that makes thighs look heavier comes from too much sitting and not enough exercising.

I think using a stationary bicycle is one of the best ways to firm up all the leg muscles. Pedalling against progressive resistance really puts your legs through their paces, and at the same time gives you an aerobic workout that burns up 3 calories a minute. My second choice would be running on a treadmill, preferably one with an adjustable incline so you can control your progress.

There's no sensible way to use barbells or dumbbells to exercise your legs. You need leverage to flex your legs with weights, which means some kind of machine. Nautilus and the others make endless types, and it seems there's one for every individual muscle in

the leg. Most aren't practical for the home gym, though. You can certainly achieve your leg-toning goals with a leg curl or leg flexion machine (see the equipment section for a rundown on the types that are available).

## BACK PAINS

We really subject our backs to terrific abuse every day by lifting things (usually the wrong way), slouching, sleeping on saggy mattresses, hunching over typewriters. It's no wonder that nearly 30 million Americans suffer from aching backs.

Correcting some bad habits can help, but there's no way of relieving your back of all the stresses it must endure. Part of the back's job is supporting the body, so it's working even when you're standing still.

One good way to take a load off your back, believe it or not, is to exercise your stomach muscles. A strong abdomen can help the back carry its burden. When the stomach muscles are weak, the back has to pick up their slack. So if you do any new model, which usually seems to cost about $50. It's hard for me to share the excitement, since I paid less than $10 at a discount store for my favorite pair.

Some people like to do their light floor exercises and stretches in bare feet. I don't see any problem in that, although if you're going to be lifting weights or using a stationary bike or other equipment, I'd strongly suggest wearing sneakers or lightweight aerobic shoes with non-slip soles.

For running regularly on a treadmill or outdoor jogging, sturdy shoes are required. The shoes should be firm, but still bend, and have a padded sole. Several of the larger runner's magazines conduct yearly tests of jogging shoes.

The socks you wear with your shoes should be made of an absorbent fiber like cotton or wool. If moisture is allowed to collect it will cause friction, which leads to blisters. I like thick wool socks, but they're too rough on my skin, so I wear a thin cotton pair underneath. Avoid colored socks; the dyes in them can infect blisters.

• *Shirts and shorts*—Any style goes here, as long as it's not so loose it can catch on equipment, or so tight it restricts your movements or chafes. Again, the material should be a natural blend that will breathe and allow moisture to escape. Your body cools itself by the evaporation of sweat from the skin. Any material that restricts evaporation will contribute to your overheating. Particularly dangerous are "sauna suits" that trap sweat between the body and a plastic fabric. Body temperatures can climb dangerously high inside these worthless garments, putting a severe strain on the heart.

Cotton fleece or cotton blend

of the exercises recommended earlier to tone up your stomach, you'll be doing your back a favor at the same time.

Be forewarned, though, that working with weights can cause more problems than it solves if you don't learn to lift properly. Keep your legs shoulder-width apart and bend down to grasp weights with your knees, not your back. Keep the weights as close to your body as possible, and lift using your knees and arms only, keeping your back straight all the time.

▶ *THE ELEGANT SUPPORT*

CREATIVE SUPPORT SYSTEMS
225 W. YANONALI ST.
SANTA BARBARA, CA 93101
(805) 965-8288

PRICE: $32.45 POSTPAID

Although it looks like a tank top, the Elegant Support is actually an exercise bra. It's made of 94 percent nylon and 6 percent Spandex to support the breasts and hold them close

to your body. The wide, crisscross straps distribute weight across a large area and there are no hooks to gouge your back. It comes in black and bright blue.

sweatsuits are fine in the colder months, but they aren't really necessary at any other time. If you need to wear one, make sure that the elastic cuffs and waistband aren't so tight that they restrict blood flow to your extremities. The same goes for leotards and tights.

- *Gloves*—Gloves aren't necessary for most workouts, but if you plan to lift weights, especially free weights, they can help you get a better and safer grip on the bar and prevent blisters. You can buy special leather weight-lifting gloves with padded palms in sporting goods shops, or by mail order through ads in fitness and body-building magazines.

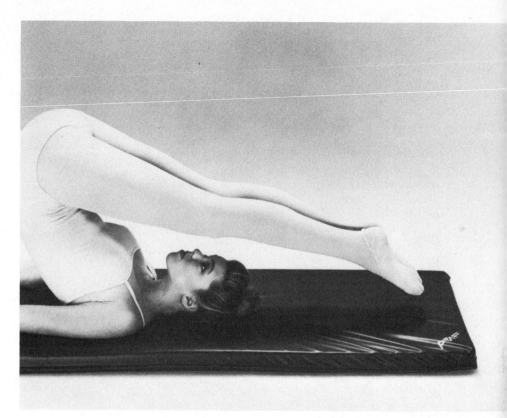

### ▶ *HOME EXERCISE MAT*
### *Model 451-100*

AMF AMERICAN
200 AMERICAN AVE.
JEFFERSON, IA 50129
(800) 247-3978

PRICE: $24.95
OPTION: SUEDED FABRIC
            COVERING—$15

A 2-by-6-foot non-folding mat that's made of thick blue vinyl filled with a 2-inch layer of urethane foam. It's sized about right for stretching, sit-ups and push-ups. For tumbling and other free-form exercises you'll need a bigger mat, which AMF makes up to 6-by-12-foot.

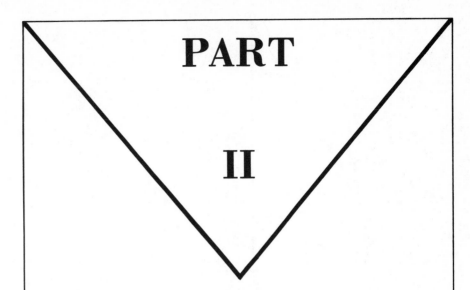

# PART

## II

# THE
# EQUIPMENT

# PUTTING YOUR GYM TOGETHER

There's never been a better time to buy home gym equipment. A few years ago home fitness equipment meant stationary bikes and free weights, and that's all you were likely to find at your local department store. Most of the more sophisticated machines were made only for institutional use and were priced out of the range most of us could afford.

When the demand for better equipment began to grow, the market exploded. Companies that never made an exercise machine that sold for less than $5,000 began developing less expensive versions for the home market. Today, with nearly 20 percent of all adults doing some kind of exercise at home, you can walk into just about any department store and find 50 types of exercise devices—everything from multi-station gyms to treadmills and rowing machines. And you can choose from three or four times that many at the "shape shops" that have sprung up around the country to sell nothing but fitness equipment. In fact, there are so many brands and models for sale these days that it's getting tough to wend your way intelligently through the chrome and Naugahyde jungle out there. What's the *real* difference between a $2,000 circuit weight trainer and one that sells for $600? How do you tell which features are actually necessary to make a stationary bike good and which are just for show?

The following chapters were written to point you in the right direction. During the past year I've spent countless hours in gyms, chain stores, sporting goods shops, and on the phone with manufacturers in an effort to sort things out. The equipment I've chosen to feature is by no means everything that's available. There are more than 70 makers of stationary bikes alone, each selling an average of five or six models. But I offer what I think is a pretty good cross section for your consideration.

From my research and an informal poll of home gym owners and dealers, I've come up with some answers to the most commonly asked questions about equipment. If you have others I suggest writing or calling the customer service department of any of the manufacturers listed in the book. They should be glad to help.

## ○ HOW DO I JUDGE QUALITY?

Often it doesn't take any more than a good look at the equipment. After you shop around and see enough of it, you'll be able to spot shoddy workmanship immediately. The use of lightweight sheet metal or lots of plastic parts are usually dead giveaways. Look closely, too, at the display models on the floor. They often get a fair amount of abuse from curious customers, and how they hold up in the store is an indication of how long they'll last in your home. I was shocked to find that at least 10 percent of the equipment I found in department stores already had broken parts.

Don't be fooled by lots of shiny chrome. It's cheap for a maker to apply a thin coat to dazzle buyers. An inexpensive chrome job sometimes start flaking off the first time you use the equipment. That's another thing to check on when inspecting floor samples.

While you're poking and probing, make sure that the display in the store doesn't give you a false impression of how the equipment works. For example, pulley weight units that can only be used if mounted with brackets on a wall are frequently exhibited in a temporary frame that makes them look like they're freestanding.

I wouldn't buy any piece of equipment that I hadn't tried out first. Most people I talked to bought something because they'd tried it out at a friend's and liked it. But don't be afraid to put the machine through its paces in the store. I've even tried out inversion racks in the middle of a crowded showroom. Better to put on a little public show than to discover a product's shortcomings after you've gotten it set up at home.

## ○ WHERE ARE THE BEST PLACES TO BUY?

You can't beat the chain stores for the biggest savings. The prices listed in this book are suggested retail. That's based on a 50 to 100 percent markup. There's no good reason why you should have to pay that. Some chain stores work on a profit margin of less than 10 percent. Consider, as one example, the Amerec 610 rowing machine. The manufacturer lists it at $350, but I've got a newspaper ad for a national store in front of me that's offering it for $249.

Don't expect much in the way of informed help from the salespeople. They do their best, but it's hard to be conversant on a dozen types of circuit trainers and treadmills when you've also got to sell hunting rifles and fishing rods. More than once I've even found that the equipment in these stores had been assembled wrong.

Sporting goods and fitness specialty shops deal in a smaller volume that forces them to charge about a 30 to 40 percent markup. In return for the premium prices, at a sporting goods or specialty shop it's more likely that you'll be dealing with someone who knows and even uses the equipment being sold. The selection is almost always better, too. When you buy a big-ticket item at one of these stores you can usually cajole someone there into coming out to the house to set it up for you. If your conscience can stand it, shop at the specialty stores but buy where you get the best price.

○ **WHAT ABOUT THE MAIL-ORDER ADS I SEE IN MAGAZINES?**

It's possible to save money buying through the mail, especially if you're dealing directly with the manufacturer. Not long ago the California maker of the $3,995-retail Heart Mate exercise bike offered it from the factory for $1,000 less. Shipping charges to Pennsylvania where I live would have added another $95, but I would have saved more than twice that on sales tax.

Some companies like Soloflex sell their product only by mail. I have major misgivings about purchasing any equipment without trying it first, and returning defective units can be a hassle.

In any case, reading the ads in magazines like *Shape* and *Muscle & Fitness* (both published by muscle maven Joe Weider of Woodland Hills, California) is a good way to keep up on the latest products and learn about health at the same time.

○ **CAN I RENT?**

Maybe. Some furniture-rental stores have added fitness equipment to their stock. They'll deliver to your house and pick it up again when you're done, provided you sign a contract for a minimum rental period. I don't think it would pay to rent any piece of equipment that sells for under $1,000, but it might be helpful if you're planning to spend big money and want to see first if you can live with the equipment.

Another way to ''rent'' is to take advantage of a trial membership at a health club. Sign on for a month or two—long enough to give all their machines a try. Better clubs have a wide selection of high-quality equipment. And if you're lucky there may even be a qualified trainer there to teach you how to use it.

○ **DO I NEED A LOT OF EQUIPMENT?**

Not at all. Most experts advise starting small and adding new pieces of equipment only as your fitness progresses.

A set of barbells will

teach you the basics of weight lifting and give you a preview of how this type of exercise will change your body. If you like what you see and feel, later you can graduate to more sophisticated weight-training machines. Free weights, a stationary bike, a rowing machine, and a treadmill or other aerobic exerciser are a good beginning for a complete whole-body fitness center.

Buy the best equipment you can afford right from the beginning. In my opinion there's no such thing as a good $75 stationary bike. The experience of using one of these rattletraps can turn you off to exercise. A decent one may cost you three times that much or more—and be worth every cent.

I spoke to one woman in Florida who managed to outfit her entire home gym with professional-quality equipment by buying it at auction. A local health club went out of business, and its creditors put lock, stock and towels on the block. Some clubs sell used equipment privately when they trade up, but you've got to figure that by then it must have taken some heavy abuse.

Finally, keep an eye on the classified ads in your newspaper. I've seen some good buys on top-of-the-line equipment in my local paper.

# STATIONARY BIKES

Americans spent $400 million on stationary exercise bikes in 1981, according to a *Newsweek* estimate. That would make these devices far and away the most popular indoor exercise equipment. But there's more to the story than the statistics indicate. The money spent on stationary bikes doesn't necessarily correlate with how regularly they are used. In far too many cases the bikes were brought home and used for a few weeks; then, as the owners grew bored or dissatisfied with them, they were shunted off to a closet or basement to accumulate dust.

That's really a shame, because stationary bicycling is fine exercise and about as safe as it comes. It can really help streamline calves, thighs and buttocks in a short time. In a University of Wyoming test, bicycling 30 minutes a day for only six weeks made the leg muscles of the 11 participants measurably more efficient. A followup showed that the blood supply and fuel-producing systems in the muscles increased by 35 percent.

For aerobic fitness, the most important type, biking, even if you're going nowhere, is on a par with swimming and running. And a relatively leisurely pace of 10 mph will consume about 200 calories per hour.

The reason most people abandon their bikes isn't

because it doesn't feel good *after* they exercise, but because it's no fun *while* they're working out. The problem can almost always be traced to poor-quality equipment. Most cheap bikes are just plain frustrating to use. They wobble and shake, have uneven pedal movement and are too noisy. A lot of them deserve to be put away somewhere.

Sporting goods dealers tell me that a few years ago the average customer spent about $100 on a stationary bike. Now, they say, the norm has risen to the $200 to $250 range. Clearly, consumers are finding that it pays to buy quality bikes. And the dealers say they get far fewer complaints when they sell the higher ticket equipment.

I don't recommend buying any bike, even an expensive one, sight-unseen. The only way to judge whether it will meet your particular needs is to try it first. Most fitness shops and even some department stores carry an extensive line of stationary bikes. Shop in sneakers and loose clothing and try a number of bikes. Don't just hop on and hop off; pedal for a few minutes and really get the feel of things. Once you've decided, you can always buy the bike by mail if you can get a better price that way.

The majority of exercise bikes are the single-action type. They're essentially scaled-down bikes with a flat base instead of a rear wheel and a seat and handlebars that don't move. A few models are dual-action and have handlebars, and sometimes seats, that move back-and-forth as you pedal, sort of combination bikes and rowing machines. Since your arms will only be following the mechanical action of the handles, there's very little upper body strength to be gained from these, but they can give you a light stretching. Just make sure that the rowing motion doesn't detract from the real reason you're there: to gain aerobic fitness by pumping the pedals.

In recent years both *Bicycling* magazine and *Consumer Reports* have tested more than a dozen stationary bikes in their labs. I've tried quite a few myself, although more informally. From their research and my own, here are some basic points to keep in mind when you're in the market for a stationary bike:

▶ *A smooth ride*—You should be doing all the moving during a workout. The bike should remain firmly in place. A sturdy frame won't flex or wobble under your weight. Don't consider a bike that isn't rock-steady, even when you're pedalling hard.

A bike's front wheel, or flywheel, can also contribute to the smoothness of the ride. Inexpensive bikes almost always have only a lightweight, spoked wheel with a plastic tire. The problem with these, according to *Consumer Reports,* is that they develop almost no momentum. When you stop pedalling, the wheel stops turning. As a result, the machines slow down or stall as the pedals reach the top and bottom of their cycle. There's no momentum to carry the pedals over the top and as a result, the action is jerky.

To that I'll add that wheels with exposed spokes can be dangerous if you have small children or pets. My cat nearly lost a paw once when his curiosity got the better of him while watching the wheel spin around on one of my early stationary bikes.

Some better bikes have weighted tires or a heavy, cast-metal flywheel up front. These do develop some momentum and are both smoother and more like using a real bicycle.

▶ *Adjustable resistance*— Thankfully, nearly all of the early exercise bikes without resistance devices have disappeared from the marketplace. Increasing the resistance against a bike's wheel is the only way to progressively build up your workload and achieve the training effect at your targeted heart rate. Resistance is supplied

to bike wheels in several ways. Some have a simple roller that rubs against the wheel. Others use caliper brakes like those on regular bikes. Machines with solid flywheels usually have a nylon strap around the outside that supplies friction. Whatever the brake type, the adjustment controls should be within easy reach and provide a wide and progressive range of resistance. You ought to be able to increase the resistance just a tiny bit if you want to. The less intricate mechanisms have only two adjustments—easy and hard—with little in between. Avoid them.

▶ *Meters*—All the stationary bikes I've used have a speedometer or tachometer to help the user pedal at an even rate. Odometers are standard equipment, too, although the number of miles you "travel" isn't nearly as important as how hard you work while logging them. The built-in pulse meters or heart monitors on

expensive bikes offer much more useful information. Some even beep to give you a goose if your heart rate falls below a present level.

▶ *Seat and handlebars*— Fanny fatigue is a common complaint among bikers, the result of seats that seem to have been designed for some other life form. A reasonably wide and well-padded seat will keep you using the bike for long workouts. Since all posteriors are not created equal, it's entirely possible that you'll find a bike that would be perfect if it weren't for the seat. Before you walk away from it, check to see if the seat can be replaced with one that fits you better.

The seat should be adjustable for height, too, since chances are more than one person in the family will want to use it. If you're tall, be sure the seat will go up high enough for you to fully extend your legs while pedalling. It's better exercise that way, and you won't get cramped from keeping your knees bent all the time. *Consumer Reports* advises setting the seat at the rider's crotch-to-floor measurement, plus two inches. Finally, don't buy a bike that has a seat that moves either sideways or up and down when the adjustment screw is fully tightened.

Adjustable handlebars are a plus in that they allow you to customize the bike to your riding position, but this isn't often a crucial factor. I've found the comfort of the hand grips to be more important. Ones made of foam are more comfortable for me than hard plastic grips.

▶ *Pedals*—I like to jump on my stationary bike at odd times when I have a few minutes to kill. Sometimes it's a bother to have to go and put on a pair of sneakers, so I prefer broad, smooth pedals that are comfortable to stockinged feet. Few bikes come with these pedals, but they can easily be installed on most. Most bike shops carry a good selection.

Some bikes are equipped with cloth or leather straps to help keep your feet in place, and a few even have metal cages like racing bikes. All do their job well and are excellent accessories. Like pedals, you can buy and install your own if they're not standard equipment.

▶ *Noise*—Without some external stimulation, stationary biking can be boring. Most people find something to occupy themselves with while riding—reading a book on a rack, watching TV, listening to music and the like. Noisy bikes are an unwelcome distraction. I've yet to find one that's silent, but some are obtrusively loud *(Consumer Reports* measured a noise level of 78 decibels at a distance of 3 feet from one they tested). The racket frequently is the result of ill-fitting parts and poor craftsmanship. It's one indicator, though not an infallible one, of quality.

Motorized exercise bikes tend to be the loudest, but that's the least important reason not to buy one. A better one is the fact that they're no good for you. When electricity is doing all the work, you're just along for the ride and you won't even be breathing hard after 20 minutes. Why waste your time? You might turn the tables and *produce* some energy rather than using it. A publishing executive I knew hooked a generator to the wheel of his stationary bike and cranked out enough power during his sessions to run a small portable TV.

### ▸ RABBIT HOME CYCLE

#### Model 510

LECO INTERNATIONAL
48 BURD ST.
NYACK, NY 10960
(914) 358-6770

PRICE: $113.60

The only reason I'm including this inexpensive Italian bike is that I like its looks so much. All the metal parts are matte black, set off by a bright yellow seat, hand grips and pedal straps. Otherwise it's the typical, low-end bike: adjustable seat and handlebars, roller brake with screw-type tension adjustment and ball-

bearing pedals. A speedometer is available for less than $10.

### ▸ SWEDISH FLYWHEEL BIKE

#### Model PVI404

THE SHARPER IMAGE
PO BOX 26823
SAN FRANCISCO, CA 26823
(800) 344-4444

PRICE: $116.50

A sleek, inexpensive folding bike. It's made of 14-gauge steel and has telescoping handlebars and an English-style seat that can be raised to accommodate people up to 6 feet 4 inches tall. The tension knob for the 20-pound flywheel is conveniently located on the angle-adjustable handlebars along with a speedometer and odometer.

This is a well-made bike, but it's mainly for people who don't have room for a larger, non-folding model.

### ▸ RACER-MATE II

#### Model 520

RACER-MATE, INC.
3016 N.E. BLAKELY ST.
SEATTLE, WA 98105
(800) 522-3610

PRICE: $119.95

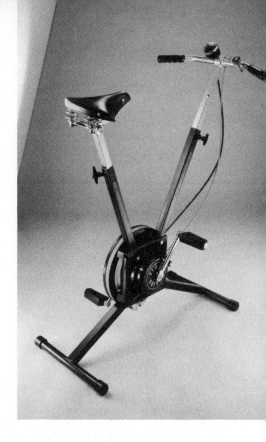

Most stationary bikes will give you a good workout, but they can't really simulate the workload of riding a real bike outdoors. That's because when you're not going anywhere, there's no headwind. And it's the resistance of the wind, along with resistance from the road, that puts the effort into bike riding.

The Racer-Mate II mechanically recreates wind resistance. It was designed to help bike racers train in bad weather and can be useful to recreational riders as well. The device consists of a stand to hold your own bike, with front wheel

removed, and a roller
mechanism with two
cylindrical fans which are
turned by the bike's rear
tire. The faster you pedal,
the more drag the fans
produce.

When *Bicycling*
magazine tested the Racer-
Mate II, they found the bike
stand to be very stable and
reported that the device did
a good job of simulating an
on-the-road feel.

An optional monitor
($49.95) attaches to the post
between the front forks of
the bike. It measures both
your horsepower output
and speed.

*Vitamaster*
MODEL# RC-PX26

▶ *ROWER EXERCISE CYCLE*

### Model BH-17

MCA SPORTS
689 FIFTH AVE.
NEW YORK, NY 10022
(800) 423-6637

PRICE: $219

A cover-flywheel bike with handlebars that have rowing action. The two functions are separate and each have their own tension controls, so you can do one or the other alone, if you like. It comes with a speedometer/odometer and timer. The oversized, 4-inch-thick padded seat is very comfortable.

▶ *SLENDERCYCLE*

### Model RC-PX26

VITAMASTER INDUSTRIES
455 SMITH ST.
BROOKLYN, NY 11231
(212) 858-0505

PRICE: $190

The Slendercycle is a smallish bike, well made but not very fancy. Its front wheel has exposed spokes and resistance is supplied by a roller-type brake with its control low on the frame. The handlebars have a convenient quick-release adjustment screw to change their angle. The fairly large, well-padded seat has a similar adjustment mechanism. When *Consumer Reports* tested this bike, they judged the smoothness of its pedal action somewhat worse than average.

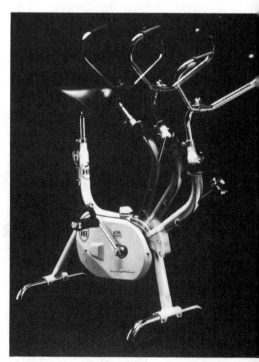

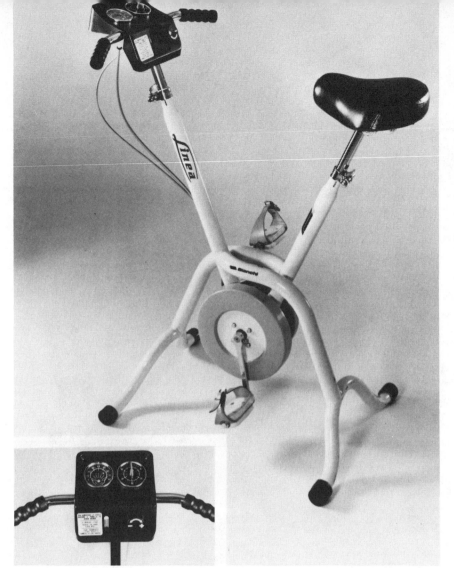

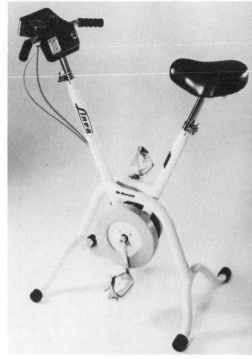

### ▶ *BIANCHI EXERCISER*

VESPA OF AMERICA CORP.
355 VALLEY DRIVE
BRISBANE, CA 94005
(415) 468-0400

PRICE: $250

Bianchi is a famous Italian maker of racing and touring bikes. This is their only stationary model. The flywheel is between the pedals rather than in front of them so there's no drive chain needed. The wheel is geared for resistance adjustment. The seat and handlebars move up and down, and the V-shaped frame can be widened or narrowed to fit your body. The whole thing folds up like a pair of scissors for storage. A speedometer, odometer and resistance knob are located between the handlebars.

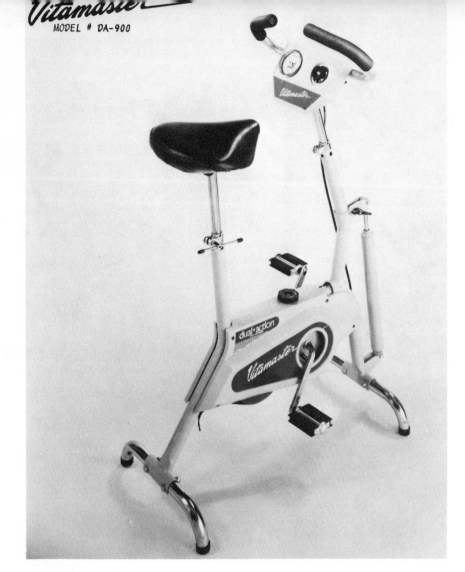

### ▶ DUAL ACTION EXERCISER

### Model DA-900

VITAMASTER INDUSTRIES
455 SMITH ST.
BROOKLYN, NY 11231
(212) 858-0505

PRICE: $270

This bike offers regular pedalling action and/or rowing action. The handlebars have a shock absorber–type tension device that allows you to push them forward and pull them back against resistance. If you prefer just to pedal, the handlebar support locks in place with a wing nut. Since the rowing and pedalling actions are separate, you can choose to do one or the other if you like. The full rowing motion requires bending forward quite sharply in the seat; some users might find this a little tough on the back.

### ▶ CARROUSEL JOGGER

### Model 616

WALTON MANUFACTURING CO.
106 REGAL ROW
DALLAS, TX 75247
(214) 637-2500

PRICE: $279

Look ma, no seat! The Carrousel Jogger is used standing up for exercise that's closer to running in place than cycling. The wide pedal platforms rotate in a 13-inch-diameter circle, which forces you to lift each leg about 10 inches per stride. Once you get some practice pedalling without holding onto the handlebars, it isn't hard to do.

One big drawback to this machine is that it's not possible to adjust the resistance on the pedals. The only way to keep a progressive training program going is to increase the length of your sessions continually, which may be inconvenient.

If you prefer a more conventional stationary bike setup, an optional seat and post is available (about $20). But because sitting down will take weight off your legs, the difficulty of the exercise will decrease.

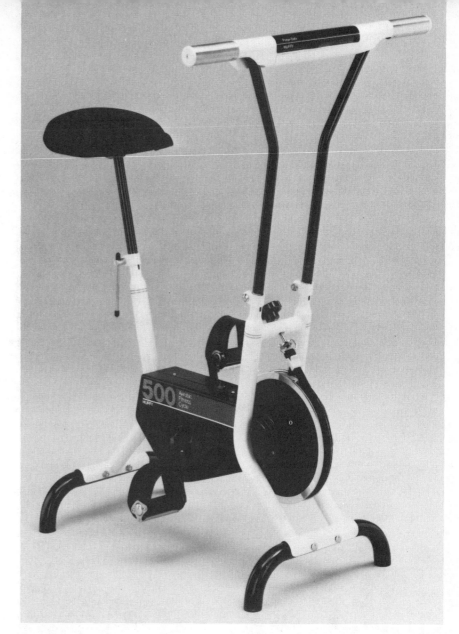

▶ *AEROBIC FITNESS CYCLE*

### *Model 90953*

HUFFY CORP.
PO BOX 07493
MILWAUKEE, WI 53207
(414) 482-4240

PRICE: $290

This is a lot of bike for the money. The 12-pound flywheel has a nylon resistance strap with easy-to-reach tension control. Ball-bearing pedals are weighted and covered, and the H-shaped frame is double bolted for rigidity. The bike comes with a built-in pulse monitor with sensors in the handlebar. The readout also shows elapsed time, speed and distance traveled in tenths of a mile.

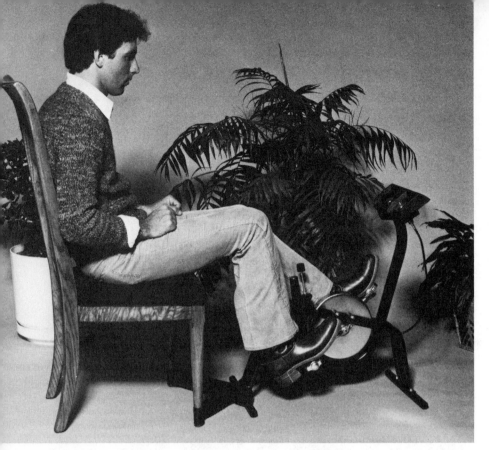

### ▶ *ADAPT-A-CYCLE*
### *Model 08611*

JAYFRO
PO BOX 400
WATERFORD, CT 06385
(203) 447-3001

PRICE: $332

The Adapt-A-Cycle has flywheel-type pedal action with adjustable tension. A set of straps allows it to be attached to any chair. This design might allow people with back and other physical problems to gain some of the benefits of stationary cycling. The unit has a speedometer and 30-minute timer and folds for storage.

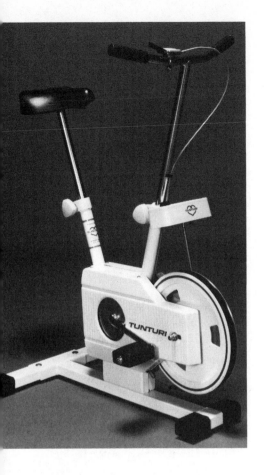

### ▶ *TUNTURI HOME CYCLE*

#### *Model ATHC*

AMEREC CORP.
PO BOX 3825
BELLVUE, WA 98009
(800) 426-0858

PRICE: $360

The Home Cycle was one of the top-rated stationary bikes in the latest *Consumer Reports* test. The magazine liked its ease of user-to-user adjustment, frame rigidity and smoothness of pedalling action. The resistance control is located right on the handlebars and the tension of the brake belt can be changed without stopping the pedals. The bike comes with a 60-minute timer with alarm and an odometer/speedometer.

### ▶ *FLEETLINE*

#### *Model FSDE-14*

JAYFRO
PO BOX 400
WATERFORD, CT 06385
(203) 447-3001

PRICE: $399

This model has a 20-inch-diameter rubber-tired wheel with covered spokes (a nice feature) and a bicycle-type brake for resistance. The pedals have wide, comfortable foot straps. Handlebars are adjustable for both height and angle. The bike comes with a speedometer and a 60-minute timer with an alarm.

### ▸ *TUNTURI ERGOMETER*

#### *Model ATEE*

AMEREC
PO BOX 3825
BELLVUE, WA 98009
(800) 426-0858

PRICE: $510

In one of its tests of stationary bikes, *Consumer Reports* gave this bike its top rating. The magazine praised the Ergometer's smooth pedalling action, resistance control,

comfortable pedals and low noise level.

It's one of the few stationary bikes that has a tachometer as well as an odometer (speedometers really don't make much sense when you're not going anywhere). This bike is also available in "racing" model ($675) with dropped handlebars, springless saddle seat and "rat trap" metal cages around the pedals.

### ▸ *SCHWINN AIR-DYNE*

EXCELSIOR FITNESS
EQUIPMENT CO.
613 ACADEMY DRIVE
NORTHBROOK, IL. 60062
(312) 291-9100

PRICE: $595

The first time I climbed onto the seat of an Air-Dyne, I fell in love. It wasn't an attraction based on looks, since this bike can be uncharitably described as big, rugged and ugly. What captured me was its spirit. It's among the most challenging, and forgiving, bikes around, unusual and fun to use.

That big caged thing up on the front of the Air-Dyne is exactly what it appears to be: a fan. Its purpose is to create drag, or resistance, while giving a very smooth feel to the pedals. It also produces a stiff breeze to cool you while you ride (there's an optional deflecting fender available for $9.95 if you prefer not to have the wind in your face all the time).

For upper-body exercise, the Air-Dyne's handlebar levers move back and forth and can power the fan without the pedals. In the middle of your ride you can put your feet up on the foot rests above the pedals and really give your arms and back a workout.

There are no resistance adjustment settings on the bike; they aren't necessary. The faster you pedal the more drag is created and the harder the work becomes. A workload indicator numbered one to seven keeps track of your output. There are two odometers, one for the "trip" mileage and the other for cumulative mileage, as well as a digital elapse timer.

Schwinn offers a "no time limit" warranty on parts and a 30-day warranty on parts and labor. I know people who have put more than 6,000 miles on an Air-Dyne without ever needing to have the bike repaired.

I do have a couple of complaints about the bike, though. For one thing, there's no way to stop the pedals or handlebars manually—you have to wait until they run out of momentum by themselves. If you want to get off before then you've got to do an adroit dismount to avoid getting whacked in the heel by the moving pedals. While the fan is a real innovation, it does create quite a whirring racket. If you want to watch TV while exercising you'll really have to turn the volume up.

### ▶ EXERCYCLE ERGOMETER

EXERCYCLE CORP.
667 PROVIDENCE ST.
WOONSOCKET, RI 02895

PRICE: $639

The Exercycle Ergometer ends up in a lot of health clubs and sports training gyms because of its durability and precise controls. The very tall handle that adjusts the tension belt on the flywheel is always within reach and, thanks to a unique pendulum device, is capable of very accurate calibrations. A patented locking mechanism keeps the belt from slipping once the tension is set. In addition, the bike has an 11-position seat post and handlebars that are adjustable with the turn of a knob. The pedals have a strap on each side to accommodate smaller and larger feet.

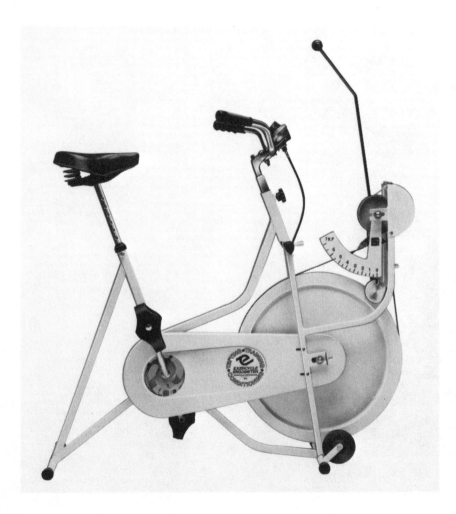

### ▶ MONARK MARK II
### *Model 0865*

UNIVERSAL FITNESS PRODUCTS
20 TERMINAL DRIVE SOUTH
PLAINVIEW, NY 11803

PRICE: $675

Made in Sweden, the Monark Mark II is an exceptionally smooth-riding bike thanks to its solid-steel flywheel and nylon belt brake. The seat is available in three sizes: wide, extra-wide and racing saddle, and the height adjustment is long enough to accommodate even very tall people. I particularly like the C-shaped handlebars which can be gripped six different ways and tilted to any angle (racing handlebars are also available). The pedals are extra wide and soft enough for bare feet but lack straps. The control panel behind the wheel houses a tall tension control, a watt meter (to measure energy output), speedometer and 30-minute timer.

### ▶ *PRO-1000*

VITAMASTER INDUSTRIES
455 SMITH ST.
BROOKLYN, NY 11231
(212) 858-0505

PRICE: $675

The major difference between this and other flywheel-type bikes in its class is the addition of an electronic console located between the handlebars. In bright red LED lights it keeps track of how long you've been exercising, what speed you've been going, the distance you've traveled, how many calories you've burned and how many you *will* burn if you keep up the same pace for an hour. By placing a finger on the built-in sensor that juts out from one side of the handlebars, you can also learn your pulse rate (you'll have to keep the finger reasonably still to get an accurate reading). All the functions are set to read out at 8-second intervals or, if you choose, you can hold any one function on the screen for as long as you like.

## ▶ LOUNGERCYCLE I
### *Model 05736*

JAYFRO
PO BOX 400
WATERFORD, CT 06385
(203) 447-3001

PRICE: $749

If you've got to exercise, you might as well be comfortable. This thickly-padded lounge chair has a flywheel-type "bike" in front and two sets of retractable pulleys on its sides.

The pedals have adjustable tension and a speedometer/odometer. One set of pulleys comes up from around your thighs; the others are pulled from behind your shoulders. They have only one resistance setting, the

equivalent of 25 pounds.

When you're not using the chair to exercise there's a padded ottoman that covers the bike portion. But even then, you're not going to be able to pass it off as just another piece of furniture—your friends are bound to wonder about those handles on the sides.

## ▶ FITRON

CYBEX
2100 SMITHTOWN AVE.
RONKONKOMA, NY 11779
(516) 585-9000

PRICE: $1,095

According to the manufacturer, the Fitron is used by more professional athletes than any other stationary bike. It's certainly a complex piece of machinery. You can preset the speed at which you want to exercise, and the bike makes you stick to it. If you try to pedal faster you can't. The more effort you put into pushing the pedals, the more resistance they develop. The speed setting can be varied so you can interval train at alternately low- and high-intensity levels.

The bike works on a hydraulic system that requires no calibration or routine maintenance. It comes with toe clips to secure your feet, and the handlebars can be reversed to simulate a racing bike position.

### ▶ ELECTRONIC ERGOMETER

#### Model EL-400

AMEREC
PO BOX 3825
BELLEVUE, WA 98009
(800) 426-0858

PRICE: $1,650

This machine seems to have been designed primarily for use in medical fitness testing, but it would make a first-rate home bike if you were willing to spend the money.

In place of the usual mechanical resistance controls is an electronically controlled electric brake that you can set to regulate the pedalling efficiency from 30 to 120 rpm. By clipping on an ear lobe sensor (not an especially comfortable item), you can watch your pulse rate continually displayed on an LED meter between the adjustable handlebars. The control panel includes a stop watch, speed indicator and efficiency control, and a quartz metronome that gives an audible beat from 40 to 200 signals a minute to pace yourself by. The Electronic Ergometer's comfortable padded seat has a gas-filled shock absorber base that can be adjusted to 40.2 inches from the pedals.

▶ *LIFECYCLE*

### Model 5000

LIFECYCLE INC.
10 THOMAS RD.
IRVINE, CA 92714
(714) 859-1011

PRICE: $1,995

The makers of the Lifecycle prefer the term "aerobic trainer" to exercise bike when describing their product. For 2,000 bucks you can call it Ralph if you want to.

Granted, this is no ordinary stationary bike. It's got a little microchip brain (powered by your pedalling) that performs numerous high-tech feats. Based on your heart rate, the computer designs an exercise program tailored to your fitness level. It automatically adjusts resistance for a warm-up period, then takes you on a trip, simulating hills and valleys. A little graphic display tells you which terrain you're on at the moment and what to expect. At the end of the ride the microprocessor remembers to give you a gradual cool-down. If you want, the machine can be switched to "manual" for an even-resistance workout.

While all this is going on, the large command module in front of you is reading out the calories per hour you're burning, the elapsed time, rpm's, even the approximate amount of oxygen you're consuming. Naturally, you also get a choice of colors for your bike: yellow, orange, red, blue or white.

### ▶ *AEROBIC JOYSTICK*

SUNCOM, INC.
650E ANTHONY TRAIL
NORTHBROOK, IL 60062

PRICE: $39.95

Now you can improve your cardiovascular fitness and your video game scores at the same time. The Aerobic Joystick is an adaptor that links your stationary bike with an Atari 2600, 400, 800, 1200 or Sears Telegame video game system. One end of the cord clips to the bike, the other plugs into the computer. you have to pedal to play. With all the quarters you save you can buy a Nautilus machine.

The joystick works best with car racing games like Activision's "Enduro" and "Grand Prix." The faster you pedal, the faster the cars whip around the track as you steer them with the joystick. You can play shooting games as well. Quicker pedalling gives you more missiles to blow away those alien spaceships. Naturally, you'll need your hands free to play this game so it's not recommended for bikes with moving handlebars.

### ▶ *HEART MATE*

WIMBLETON INDUSTRIES
260 W. BEACH AVE.
INGLEWOOD, CA 90302
(213) 677-8131

PRICE: $3,995

The Heart Mate is built along the lines of the Lifecycle but with two indispensable extras: a built-in color TV and AM/FM stereo to take your mind off the work. For the extra $1,000 you also get pedal straps, a heart-rate sensor, foam-padded handlebars and a clearer set of directions. By the way, in case you were wondering the TV *will* accept cable and a videotape recorder.

# FREE WEIGHTS

Free weights, barbells and dumbbells remain the cheapest body-building equipment available. For about $60 you can buy a complete free-weight set that includes bar, collars and 80 pounds of weight plates (more than enough for the average weight lifter).

You get what you pay for. Free weights are basic appliances, with limitations to go along with their relatively economical price. Physics and physiology are essentially working against free weights. Body movements are rotary in nature, but lifting barbells is a straight up-and-down motion. Consequently, during the lift muscles are exercised over a small range of their operation. When the joints are locked at the end of a lift, the bones are bearing the weight and the muscles are doing very little work.

For sports, where power over a full range of movement is needed, free weights may not be the ideal training equipment. More sophisticated pulley and Nautilus machines, which work muscles through a greater range, produce better overall fitness.

Then there's the safety factor. Whereas machines control the weight for you, free weights demand that you be in control—always. A slip when you've got 50 pounds of iron in your hands can be a dangerous one. The heavier the weight you're hoisting, the more danger there is that you'll lose your balance.

The majority of weight-lifting accidents happen to people who are alone when working out. If any significant amount of weight is involved, it's critical that a spotter be standing very close by to check your position and to grab the weights if there's trouble.

Blackouts aren't uncommon among professional weight lifters. Doctors studying the problem say that fainting spells are the result of elevated blood pressure during the lift and the tendency of the participants to hold their breath during parts of the movement. To avoid this, stick with lighter weights and lift them numerous times. And always hold the barbell in front of your body or behind it. *Never* lift weights directly above your head.

In their favor, free weights are less restrictive than machines and allow lots of movement in just about any direction. And they bring many muscles into play at the same time. You can work on just about all the major muscle groups with free weights. Legs, for example, can be firmed by standing from a squat or bent-knee position while holding a barbell or dumbbell.

Free weights are a good introduction to weight lifting, provided you get some good advice on proper lifting techniques before starting a program. Later, you may want to invest in weight benches and machines to isolate certain of your body's problem areas.

The equipment itself hasn't changed a great deal in the 80 years it's been around. The average barbell set includes a bar that's about 5 feet long and an inch in diameter weighing 20 pounds or so. It should have two knurled areas to act as grips. The round weights, or plates, slide onto the ends of the bar and are held in place with collars. On some brands the inside collar is integral and doesn't move. Most movable collars tighten down with a screw mechanism. It's a simple procedure, but not one you ever want to do in a hurry. A loose plate could slip and throw the barbell off balance, or worse, fall on your toe.

Weight sets that come in 2½- to 3-pound increments are preferable because they let you add just a little at a time as your sessions progress. Professional-type weight sets usually have solid iron plates, an advantage because they're fairly thin. But iron weights require thick mats or carpeting on the floor and understanding neighbors downstairs. Weights also come with plastic coating and rubber rings that fit around iron plates. One company even makes the plates themselves from dense rubber.

Dumbbells are scaled-down barbells used for one-hand lifting. They are very versatile, and you can work with them while sitting down if you like. They come in one-piece cast metal versions or with removable plates. Many barbell kits come with a dumbbell bar so you can utilize one set of plates for both.

### ▶ FILLABLE DUMBBELLS

**Models 216, 217 & 218**

LECO INTERNATIONAL
48 BURD ST.
NYACK, NY 10960
(914) 358-6770

PRICES: SMALL—$4.80
MEDIUM—$6.00
LARGE—$7.20

Similar to Travel Weights, these are one-piece, red dumbbells. Filled with water, the small model weighs 2.2 pounds, with sand just over 4 pounds. The medium size weighs 4½ pounds with water and 8 pounds with sand. The large size weighs 6½ pounds and 12½ pounds respectively.

### ▶ DUMBBELLS

**Models DB30 & DB50**

AMF AMERICAN
200 AMERICAN AVE.
JEFFERSON, IA 50129
(800) 247-3978

PRICES: $8.95 to $11.50

These are bright blue plastic dumbbells filled with cement. They are available in 3-, 5- and 10-pound weights.

### ▶ MUSCLE BUILDER

**Model 211**

LECO INTERNATIONAL
48 BURD ST.
NYACK, NY 10960
(914) 358-6770

PRICE: $30

Kids might find these inexpensive, fillable plastic weights fun. The kit includes bars for a barbell and two dumbbells, along with six blue plastic hollow plates. Filled with water, the whole thing weighs only 42 pounds. You can increase the weight to 100 pounds by filling them with sand instead.

### ▶ SOLID RUBBER DISCS

YORK BARBELL CO.
BOX 1707
YORK, PA 17405
(717) 767-6841

PRICES: 22-POUND DISC—$44
33-POUND DISC—$56
44-POUND DISC—$68
55-POUND DISC—$80

York Barbell originally intended these weights for use in health clubs and gyms, but now finds that a

circumference to protect your floors.

The weight rings come in 5-, 10- and 20-pound denominations, and each can fit into the housing by itself. My only complaint is that the weights don't come

significant percentage of them are going into homes. They're expensive ($200 for a 110-pound set, not including bar) but so are repairs to the wood floors they're designed to protect.

The plates are made of dense, solid rubber with a brass bushing to reinforce the hole and make removing them easier. They can be used with any 2-inch-diameter bar. Unlike metal weights, which are graduated in size according to weight, the rubber discs are all the same diameter but have varying thicknesses. The smallest weight available is 22 pounds, which means adding a minimum of 44 pounds at a time.

### ▶ POWER RINGS

SPALDING
425 MEADOW ST.,
PO BOX 901
CHICOPEE, MA 01021

PRICE: $109

Traditionally weight plates are stacked on the ends of the bar in a line, with the smallest on the outside. Spalding has come up with an entirely different design. The weights for the Power Ring system nestle inside of one another and fit into a locking housing. As a result, 35 pounds of weights will fit into a space only 2⅛-inches wide. You can put all the weight on the ends of the bar, which gives it better balance. The metal housing has a secure, screw-type lock and has a thick ring of plastic around its

in smaller increments; 10 pounds is the minimum you can add and that's a rather large jump for a progressive weight lifting regimen.

### ▶ CHROME DUMBBELLS
#### Model PVI450

THE SHARPER IMAGE
PO BOX 26823
SAN FRANCISCO, CA 94126
(800) 344-4444

PRICE: $136.50 POSTPAID

The weights and handles are triple chrome-plated and polished for looks. The set comes with 12 weight plates (four 5-, 2½- and 1¼-pound discs) for a total of 45 pounds. They come with a one-year guarantee, though I can't imagine how you could break them.

### ▶ SUPREME IRON BARBELLS
#### Model S110

BILLARD BARBELL CO.
208 CHESNUT ST.
READING, PA 19602
(215) 375-4333

PRICE: $67

A medium-priced, high-quality barbell and dumbbell set that has revolving sleeves and comes with four 10- and 5-pound plates and six 2½-pounders. The barbell has built-in wrenches for tightening; the dumbbells have small screws that lock with a wrench that's provided.

### ▶ UNIVERSAL BARBELLS
#### Model UL310

BILLARD BARBELL CO.
208 CHESNUT ST.
READING, PA 19602
(215) 375-4333

PRICE: $350

If you're planning to build your weight lifting regimen around free weights, it pays to invest in a professional set like this one. The weights are cast iron and the set includes two 45-pound and four each of 25-, 10- and 2½-pound plates. They are mounted with a universal spindle hub and a collar that clamps with two wing nuts. It takes longer to change plates

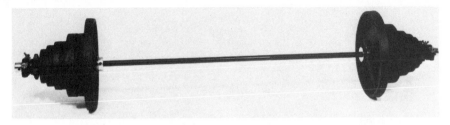

with this system, but when the weights are on, they're secure.

One important feature is that the knurled, black oxide steel bar rotates within the sleeves that the weights are on. Having a bar that turns makes some lifting movements easier.

▶ **TRICEP EXERCISER**
*Model TRE2*

BILLARD BARBELL
208 CHESNUT ST.
READING, PA 19602

PRICE: $11

One of the best exercises for triceps is performed by holding the weight straight above your head and then slowly lowering it behind your shoulders until your elbows are pointed almost straight up. Triceps bars like this one have two vertical handles in the

middle to make triceps presses more comfortable to do. Like the Tricep Exerciser, most such bars come with locking collars included but leave it to you to supply the weights.

▶ **WEIGHT LIFTING GLOVES**
*Model WLG*

BILLARD BARBELL CO.
208 CHESNUT ST.
READING, PA 19602
(215) 375-4333

PRICE: $12

Weight Lifting Gloves are designed to protect your hands and give you a better grip on the bar when using free weights. These are made of cabretta leather with reinforced palms, cotton-mesh backing and Velcro closures.

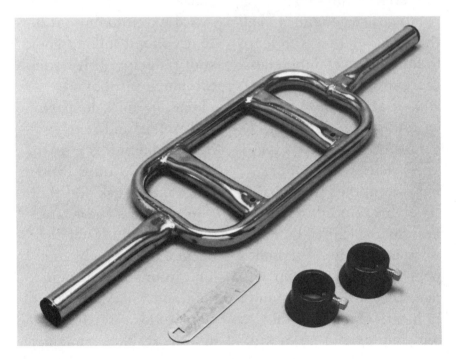

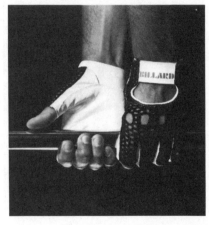

# WEIGHT BENCHES AND SPECIALTY MACHINES

Nature being as imperfect as it is, none of us is without his or her problem areas. Whether it's spindly legs, a flabby waistline, a bad back or weak, saggy arms, few of us can honestly say there's nothing we wouldn't change about our bodies. Sometimes our short-comings are genetic, and all that can be done is to learn to love our own uniqueness. More often it's a matter of lack of attention to those irritating anatomical details.

No matter what your weak area, there's probably a weight-training device designed specifically to work on it. These weight benches and single-purpose machines are usually found in health clubs, and they're only one part of an overall fitness set-up. But if you've been plagued by a body problem all your life, the chances are you'll have to work continually on it for lasting improvement. In such cases, investing in specialty equipment for a home gym makes good sense.

I'd like to point out here that I'm not talking about spot reducing. If it's simply too much fat that's to blame, no miracle machine will isolate and remove it. Spot reduction is a myth. You can do sit-ups from dawn until dusk and they won't make a spare tire disappear any faster than fat in another body area. In fact, in one experiment, men and women did up to 400 sit-ups a day for a month, yet their abdomens showed no special decrease in fat. They lost weight over their entire bodies at about the same rate.

Aside from fat, lack of muscle firmness and tone can be blamed as the cause of many spot body problems. Legs, for example, can *look* longer and sleeker after several months of weight training. Firming up arm muscles will give them better definition and more shapely lines.

One of the most popular specialty machines is the leg curl/extension machine. It's a bench with two sets of movable, padded bars at the end, attached either to free weight plates or a pulley and weight stack. To do calf-firming curls, lie on your stomach and lift the bars with the backs of your calves. For thigh-building extensions, lie on your back and lift the lower bars with the tops of your feet.

On the other end of the complexity spectrum are high-tech marvels like vertical butterfly machines, which isolate back and arm muscles, and pullover machines for building chest and pectoral muscles. The photos in this chapter do a lot better job of explaining how these complicated devices work than words can.

Most of these specialty machines are built by top-name companies such as Nautilus, Universal and Marcy. The quality and the prices are consistently high. Simple weight benches are another story. The market is crowded with manufacturers, some decidedly better than others. Be forewarned about benches made with thin metal, narrow diameter tubing. I've heard horror stories about a few of these collapsing under the combined pressure of exerciser and weights. A sturdy, heavy-gauge frame and joints that are welded rather than bolted together are two indicators of good craftsmanship. Thick vinyl padding on the bench bed and any bars and handles will make using a machine a lot more comfortable.

► *TUMMYMASTER DELUXE*

*Model 7421*

SUNBEAM LEISURE PRODUCTS CO.
HOWARD BUSH DRIVE
NEOSHO, MO 64850
(417) 451-4450

PRICE: $43

This attractive beige slant board has two padded foot rungs, a lower one for bent-knee sit-ups and an upper one for a more difficult version of the same exercise. The angle of incline is present and cannot be adjusted.

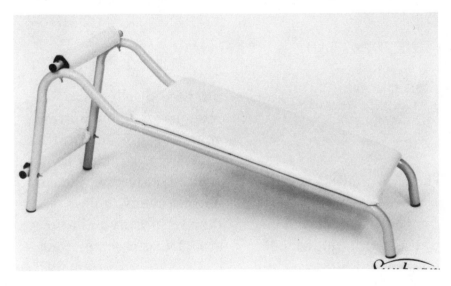

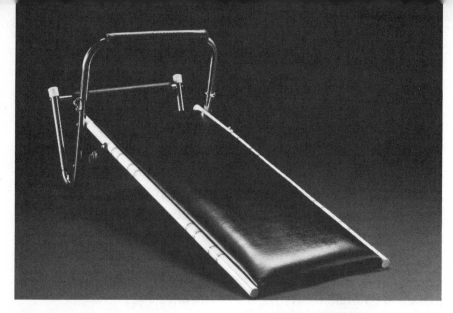

### ► HOME SLANTBOARD

#### Model SB-1

MCA SPORTS
689 FIFTH AVE.
NEW YORK, NY 10022
(800) 423-6637

PRICE: $49

This very inexpensive, three-position slant board has a 1¼-inch tubular steel frame and thick padded bars in front for doing both straight- and bent-leg sit-ups.

### ► THE DIPSTAND

M&R INDUSTRIES
9215 151st AVE. NE
REDMOND, WA 98052
(206) 885-1010

PRICE: $99

The Dipstand is used primarily for exercising arms and shoulders. You grab the two (unpadded) handles and hoist yourself

up, then do dipping motions while supporting your weight entirely with your arms. Dipping is hard work and most people can't do very many, unless they've already built up arm strength some other way.

### ► SQUAT RACK

#### Model 485

MARCY FITNESS PRODUCTS
2801 W. MISSION RD.
ALHAMBRA, CA 91803
(213) 570-1222

PRICE: $102

A squat rack is used to hold your barbell so you can get it safely positioned behind your neck for doing leg-building squats. This chrome-and-black model is made of 2-inch-diameter tubing and has diagonal brace supports. It adjusts to three positions with thick pins.

The bench is made of 1¼-inch-diameter steel tubing and has six legs for extra stability. The bench back inclines to five positions with a ⅛-inch-thick steel brace behind it. It can hold a combined weight of 500 pounds when flat and 300 pounds when inclined. The frame is painted chocolate brown and the bench cover is beige vinyl.

### ▶ *BODY BLASTER*

WEIDER HEALTH AND FITNESS
2110 ERWIN ST.,
WOODLAND HILLS, CA 91367
(213) 884-6800

PRICE: $160

Joe Weider, the man in this photo, is a very big name in body building circles. It's probably obvious from the plates he's got stacked on that barbell (I figure there's at least 300 pounds) that the Body Blaster exercise bench is being aimed at serious weight lifters. But it's a well-designed and versatile piece of equipment; with a lot less weight on it, it would nicely serve the purposes of anyone who's looking just to stay in shape.

The heavy-duty frame is made of thick steel and powder-coated to resist scratching. The vinyl-covered, padded bench has an adjustable back for incline presses and a seat that drops for leg extensions and raises for decline presses and leg curls. For the money, the Body Blaster is an excellent buy!

### ▶ *INCLINE WEIGHT BENCH*

#### *Model FSIW-3*

JAYFRO
PO BOX 400
WATERFORD, CT 06385
(203) 447-3301

PRICE: $162.50
OPTION: LEG-LIFT
       ADAPTER—$108

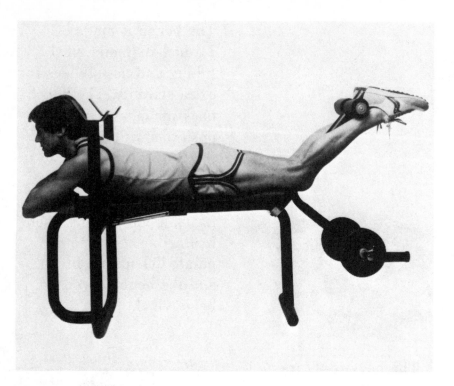

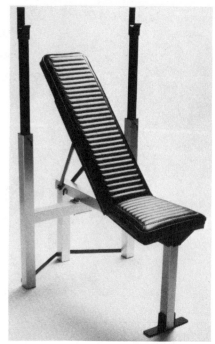

### ▶ INCLINE PRESS BENCH

### *Model 470*

MARCY FITNESS PRODUCTS
2801 W. MISSION RD.
ALHAMBRA, CA 91803
(213) 570-1222

PRICE: $191

Features of this bench
include a four-position
incline back with a self-
locking pin, an extra-wide
weight rack, a fifth leg for
added support and a 2 inch-
thick high-density foam
padding.

### ▶ LIFESTYLER WEIGHT BENCH

### *Model 700*

AMF AMERICAN
200 AMERICAN AVE.
JEFFERSON, IA 50129
(800) 247-3978

PRICE: $239
OPTION: LEG
        CURL/EXTENSION
        ATTACHMENT—$69

This weight bench is
intended for home gyms
but built with the
ruggedness of institutional
equipment. It has a heavy,
square metal frame with
weight racks that telescope
on nylon guides to adjust
from 39 to 61 inches high.
The textured vinyl bench
has 2 inches of foam
padding, and the seat
widens near the end to
make it more comfortable
when inclined. In addition,
the seat frame can be
shortened to bring you
closer to the barbell for
doing incline presses. An
optional leg station with
curl and extension modes
can be bolted onto the front
leg.

## ▶ LIFESTYLER 2000

### Model 2000

AMF AMERICAN
200 AMERICAN AVE.
JEFFERSON, IA 50129
(800) 247-3978

PRICE: $399

This wall-mounted bench uses hydraulic cylinders rather than weights for resistance. Adjusting the angle of the cylinders (12 positions) increases the resistance, up to the equivalent of 242 pounds. The machine can be used for arm and leg presses with the bench in place and squats when it's removed. The bench can be used by itself for a slant board and the whole unit folds against the wall.

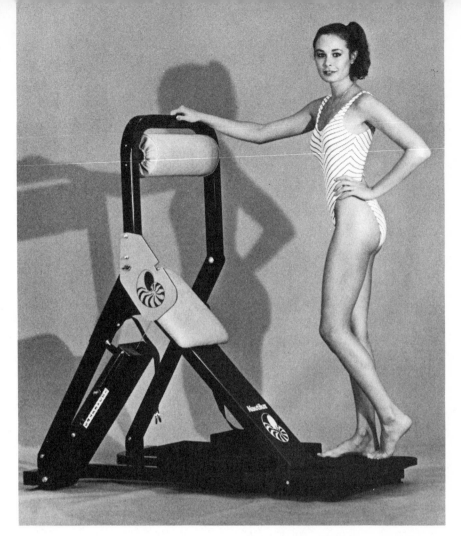

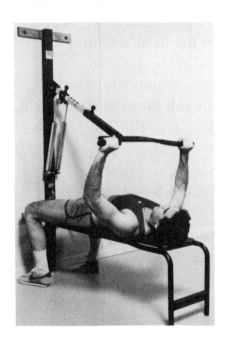

## ▶ NAUTILUS BACK MACHINE

NAUTILUS SPORTS/MEDICAL INDUSTRIES
PO BOX 1783
DE LAND, FL 32720
(800) 874-8941

PRICE: $435

This is a home gym version of Nautilus's $2,300 Lower Back Machine. It utilizes a simplified design of the famous variable-resistance cam but lacks a weight stack. Resistance is supplied by a series of strong, stretchy cords. Each number on the nine-position adjustment scale engages another cord. There's no way to tell exactly how much weight you are moving, but the maker estimates that No. 1 on the resistance scale is equal to about 20 pounds and No. 9 about 200 pounds. To use the machine, you push backwards on the padded resistance bar with your shoulders. A seat belt holds you lower body in place during the exercise.

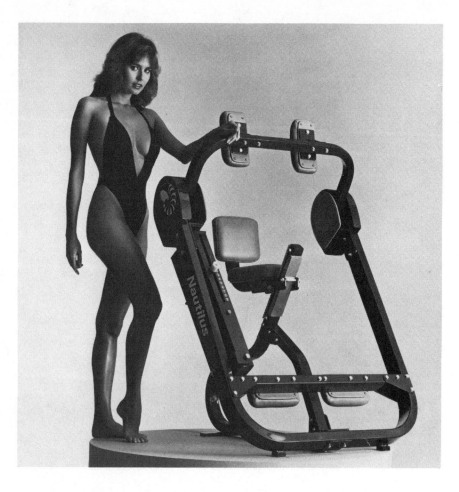

## ▶ ARM CURLING MACHINE

CORBIN-GENTRY, INC.
40 MAPLE ST.
SOMERVILLE, CT 06072
(800) 243-5728

PRICE: $565

Why bother with an expensive arm curling machine when the exercise is one of the simplest you can do with free weights? Most people don't need a single-use device like this one. But for body builders who spend a lot of time doing arm curls, it has several advantages: Its deep, upholstered pads support the elbows during the exercise to make curling easier on the joints and take some of the strain off the back. The machine's weight arms force the user to lift in an arc that balances the load proportionately through the full range of the motion. The Arm Curling Machine, which uses free-weight plates, is 49 inches tall and cannot be adjusted for height.

## ▶ NAUTILUS ABDOMINAL MACHINE

NAUTILUS SPORTS/MEDICAL
INDUSTRIES
PO BOX 1783
DE LAND, FL 32720

PRICE: $485

The Nautilus Abdominal Machine, patterned after the company's $2,500 commercial unit, works only the abdominal muscles. The exercise is performed by pushing forward on the resistance bar with your upper body. A rotary cam mechanism provides variable resistance in both directions, so abdominal muscles benefit in both the contraction and extension phases.

Like the other Nautilus home machines, this one uses round elastic cords for resistance. The tension is set with a sliding knot and can be changed in seconds.

### ▸ BICEPS/TRICEPS MACHINE

#### Model 106

HYDRA-FITNESS
2121 INDUSTRIAL BLVD.
BELTON, TX 76513
(800) 792-3010

PRICE: $650

The Hydra-Fitness Biceps/Triceps Machine utilizes dual hydraulic cylinders to supply resistance. As a result it's smooth and quiet and takes up less room than a weight machine. The machine is only 39 inches long and weighs 85 pounds.

Flexing the arms by pulling up on the top bar builds the biceps; pushing down on the lower bar strengthens the triceps. Resistance is variable from approximately 0 to 165 pounds in the biceps mode and 0 to 135 pounds in the triceps exercise.

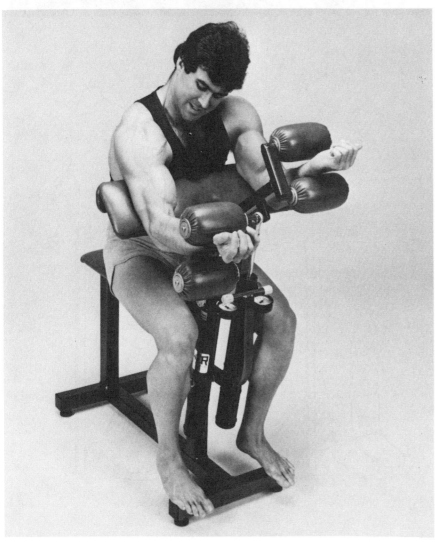

### ▶ SWEDISH TWIST STAND

#### Model 1022

HOGGAN HEALTH EQUIPMENT
6651 S. STATE ST
SALT LAKE CITY, UT 84107

PRICE: $895

Remember The Twist? Chubby Checker might have had a different nickname if he'd kept it up. Twisting your lower body is good exercise. It tones up leg and waist muscles and gets your heart pumping. Even if you can't dance, this machine makes twisting easy. There are even two identical stations so you can grab a partner and put on your old 45s.

The stainless steel handles are to hold onto so your upper body will stay straight. The revolving rubber-covered pads move on ball bearings and have a metal strap over the top to keep your feet in place.

If you haven't done much twisting lately, you should go slowly at first with a machine like this. The movement isn't one your body does very often and you could pull a muscle if you overdo it too soon.

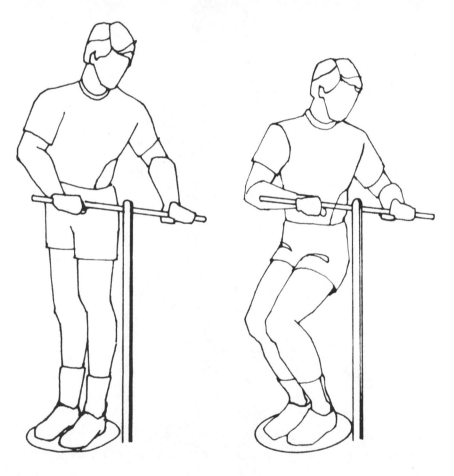

## ▶ UPRIGHT ROW/TRICEPS EXTENSION

### Model 315

HYDRA-FITNESS
PO BOX 599
BELTON, TX 76513
(800) 433-3111

PRICE: $1,270

This machine isolates the triceps, shoulder and upper chest muscles. It uses a single hydraulic cylinder for resistance in both directions. You won't know exactly how much weight you're lifting, but a gauge on the cylinder offers an estimate.

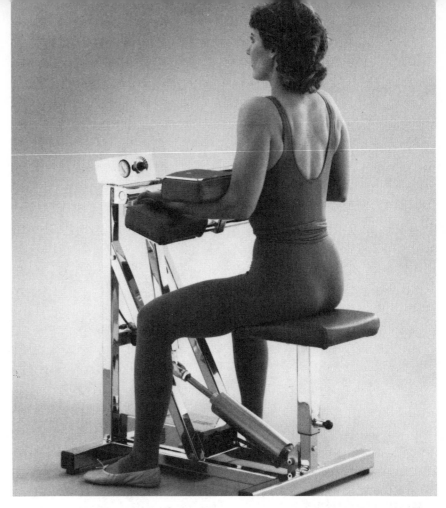

## ▶ CAM II SHOULDER SHRUG

### Model 1803

KEISER SPORTS HEALTH EQUIP.
411 S. WEST AVE.
FRESNO, CA 93706
(209) 266-2715

PRICE: $1,725

Keiser makes quality equipment that's used by many professional sports teams. Instead of weights, the machines use pneumatic cylinders for resistance. While this has many advantages such as smooth, quiet operation and infinitely variable resistance, you face the disadvantage of needing to buy a compressor ($515) to charge the cylinders.

This machine strengthens the back and shoulder muscles. To use it you move the resistance bar upward with your lower arms using a shrugging motion. The company also makes a leg extension machine ($2,240) and squat deck ($2,450), as well as other equipment. The same compressor can be used with all the machines.

If you're willing to spend $2,000 to build your shoulder and triceps muscles, this is the machine for you. To use it you adjust the seat to the proper height, grab the handles above your head and press upward, keeping your back straight. The machine comes with a 250-pound weight stack in 10-pound increments. According to *Shape* magazine, short or tall people may have trouble adjusting the seat to their height on this machine.

### ▶ ROW MACHINE
#### Model B

CORBIN-GENTRY
40 MAPLE ST.
SOMERVILLE, CT 06072
(800) 243-5728

PRICE: $1,869

Calling this a rowing machine is akin to describing the *U.S.S. New Jersey* a dinghy! This is a weight-lifting apparatus for strengthening your back, shoulders and arms. The rowing motion activates a lever that raises the weight bar. The seat, adjustable for height, remains stationary and there's a large, padded beam in front of it to keep your body in place as you pull back on one of the two sets of handlebars. Since using the Row Machine doesn't require a lot of movement, and the number of lifts you can do is limited, it doesn't offer the aerobic benefit of ordinary rowing machines.

### ▶ OVERHEAD PRESS MACHINE

NAUTILUS SPORTS/MEDICAL INDUSTRIES
PO BOX 1783
DE LAND, FL 32720
(800) 874-8941

PRICE: $2,085

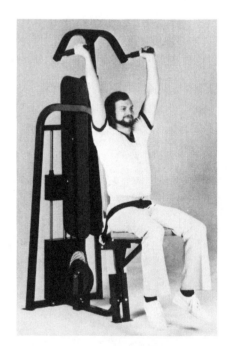

### ▶ LOWER BACK MACHINE

NAUTILUS SPORTS/MEDICAL
INDUSTRIES
PO BOX 1783
DE LAND, FL 32720
(800) 874-8941

PRICE: $2,285

The majority of people who suffer from lower back pain don't have any disease or injury, just weak muscles in that area. When the muscles go unused they lose elasticity and shorten, which cause discomfort.

Nautilus's Lower Back Machine is designed to strengthen the *erector spinae* muscles of the lower back. The large pads in front hold your legs down while you push the weight bar backwards with your upper torso. The machine comes with 250 pounds of weights in 10-pound increments. A chrome version is available for about $300 more.

### ▶ FRONTAL SHOULDER AND CHEST MACHINE

#### *Model 2090*

CAMSTAR
6651 S. STATE ST.
SALT LAKE CITY, UT 84107
(801) 266-5337

PRICE: $2,350

The CamStar 2090 isolates the *pectoralis major* (chest) and *anterior deltoid* (inner shoulder) muscles. A lot of women use machines like this, because it is the pectoral muscles that lie underneath the breasts. Exercising them won't actually make the breasts larger, but it can expand the chest and make them *look* larger and higher.

To work this machine, you adjust the seat to the proper height for you, grab the metal handles and push your inner forearms against the padded bars, trying to move them forward until your elbows touch. A gear-and-pulley mechanism transfers the resistance of the weights behind you into this forward motion.

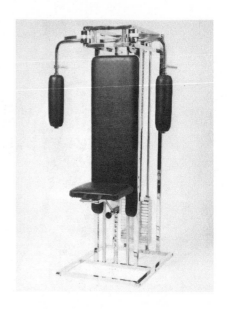

### ▶ FULL TWISTING TORSO CONDITIONER

#### *Model 2025*

CAMSTAR
6651 S. STATE ST
SALT LAKE CITY, UT 84107
(801) 266-5337

PRICE: $2,600

All this machinery just to firm up your love handles! The CamStar 2025 isolates and conditions the internal and external oblique muscles, which run between the lower ribs and the hips. It uses square weight plates and a Nautilus-style cam to

This pullover exercise isolates the muscles in the chest and upper back. Your hands rest on the curved bar, but the weights are actually moved in a circular motion with the backs of your elbows. Nautilus's cam mechanism supplies resistance throughout the entire movement. This is an incredible machine but is priced out of most people's range.

provide resistance over a full range of movement.

The idea of this exercise is to use your obliques to twist your body around 180 degrees against the weights while gripping the seat with your legs. Believe me, it's harder than it looks.

▶ *PULLOVER MACHINE*

NAUTILUS SPORTS/MEDICAL
INDUSTRIES
PO BOX 1783
DE LAND, FL 32720
(800) 874-8941

PRICE: $2,720

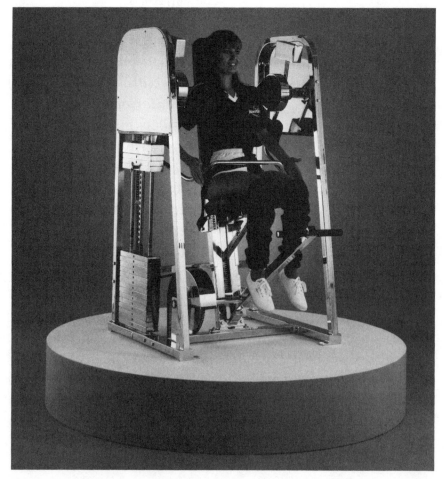

## ▶ *CHEST MACHINE*

NAUTILUS SPORTS/MEDICAL
INDUSTRIES
PO BOX 1783
DE LAND, FL 32720
(800) 874-8941

PRICE: $2,995

The Chest Machine builds up the *pectoralis major* muscles in the upper chest. The weight arms are pulled forward from behind the shoulders with the inner forearms. (The woman in the photo is at the finish position.) There are cheaper versions of this machine around, but none any better.

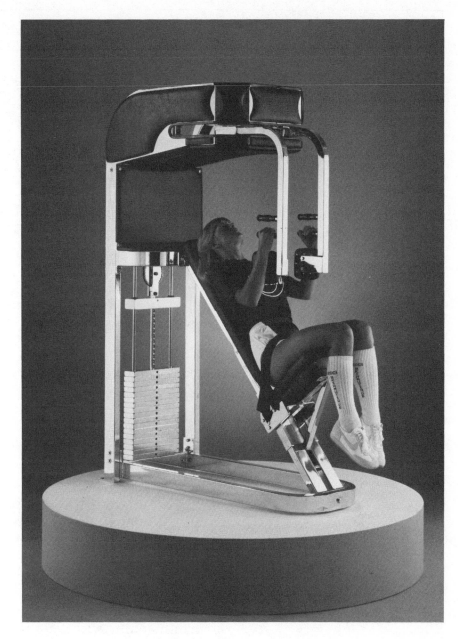

# MULTI-GYMS

They refer to it as "doing the circuit," and it's one of the best ways going to firm and shape your entire body. Circuit weight training can elevate your levels of strength, endurance, flexibility and power and at the same time sculpt fat into muscle. Unlike traditional weight training, circuit weight training also increases your cardiovascular fitness.

The equipment used for circuit training is a multi-gym, a machine with weight lifting stations each designed to exercise a specific part of the body: legs, arms, back and shoulders, chest and abdominals. Comparatively light weight or resistance settings are used—about 40 percent of the maximum you can lift—but the lift is repeated eight or ten times instead of once or twice. When the set of lifts is finished at one station, you move on to the next as soon as possible.

Most beginners in circuit training find that getting through one trip around the machine leaves them panting. But after a month or six weeks, most people can complete three circuits without stopping. Once that plateau is reached, it's just a matter of regularly increasing the amount of weight or number of repetitions to keep the training effect going.

In traditional weight lifting exercises, a heavy load is lifted several times with a long rest before the next lift. While these explosive lifts develop lots of power and are great if you throw the shot put or are a professional body builder, they don't tax the heart and lungs at all because of their short duration. Not so with circuit training. Moving quickly from station to station with only a 15-second or so rest between taxes the cardiovascular system and increases its endurance. In one study, circuit weight training increased aerobic fitness 5 percent in women and 6 percent in men. Those aren't very impressive numbers compared to a program of jogging or working out on a stationary bike, but they add up to a significant bonus from exercise that improves whole-body fitness as well.

Two other studies proved that joggers can reduce their weekly mileage by half and maintain their aerobic fitness for 5 to 15 weeks if they circuit train instead. That's good news if you have an injury or the weather turns bad for a spell.

You won't lose much actual weight through circuit training, but you'll probably look as if you did. This type of exercise turns loose flab into tight, dense muscle. When you step on the scales after a couple of months there won't be much change because the fat loss will have been offset by the muscle gain, but if you use a tape measure, the difference will be apparent. Men tend to lose inches in the thighs this way, women reduce around the middle.

Circuit training really shines when you look at the increase in strength that's possible. Some tests have shown arm and leg strength increases of 50 percent and more in people who weren't fit to begin with. Imagine being half again as strong as you are now. You could use that extra muscle power for sports, work or to just get you through all the lifting and lugging the average day.

The very best multi-gyms are professional quality— big, rugged and with all the stations laid out individually so more than one person can use them at a time. They usually include chest and shoulder presses, an overhead pulley for building the back and triceps, and leg curl or extension machines. They also cost an arm and a leg, upwards of $5,000 in some cases. Obviously that's a heavy-duty investment, but if you're committed to fitness and can afford it, the price is worth it.

Compact and less expensive multi-gyms abound. Rather than offer separate work stations, these combine all the functions in one bench. For example, when the bench is removed, the chest press becomes a squat press. Or, by raising the handlebars, it's transformed into an arm-extension machine.

Frankly, it's hard to circuit train on these cheaper gyms. For aerobic effect you shouldn't pause more than a few seconds between exercises. After that, the heart rate begins to fall and sets you back. If you must stop after each station to detach a bench or raise a bar, the momentum will be lost. Strength benefits aren't affected, however, and you can buy one of these smaller machines for about a tenth of the price of a professional unit.

Nearly all of the larger multi-gyms and most of the smaller ones use a stacking weight system for resistance. The flat, iron plates are raised and lowered by pulleys which provide maximum control and smooth action. The amount of weight is selected by moving a metal pin to isolate the number of plates you want to lift.

Some units come with chrome-plated weights, and some manufacturers such as Marcy will chrome-plate weights if you pay extra. Shiny weights and frame tubing look good but add considerable cost to a machine and serve only cosmetic purposes.

Before you buy any machine, large or small, make sure that what you see is what you'll get. The display models on showroom floors are often loaded with lots of options that aren't included in the basic price. These extras, many of them worth considering, can add $1,000 or more to the bottom line.

### ▶ *LIFESTYLER 1000*

AMF AMERICAN
200 AMERICAN AVE.
JEFFERSON, IA 50129
(800) 247-3978

PRICE: $99

An adjustable pulley-weight system that mounts on a wall, the Life Styler 1000 can be used for both arm and leg exercises by switching between the handgrip and leg cuff. The pulley mechanism slides up and down the 79-inch-high bar to make the change for upper and lower body pulls. The weight pack consists of five 5-pound plates that are color-coded. This machine is designed strictly for low-resistance, high-repetition exercise.

### ▶ *ORBIT-TRAC*
### *Model OB-1*

MCA SPORTS
689 FIFTH AVE.
NEW YORK, NY 10022
(800) 423-6637

PRICE: $129 WITHOUT
        WEIGHTS

It's basically a weight bench, but I've included the Orbit-Trac in the multi-gyms chapter because you can do so many exercises with it. By flipping the

hinged, balanced weight bar into various positions, the machine can be used for bench and triceps presses, biceps curls, squats, front raises and sit-ups. The U-shaped grip bar holds the weight so you can safely work out without a spotter.

### ▶ DELUXE FOLDAWAY

#### Model 7942

SUNBEAM LEISURE PRODUCTS CO.
HOWARD BUSH DRIVE.
NEOSHO, MO 64850
(417) 451-4450

PRICE: $180

This tubular steel, bolt-together system features a five-position incline bench and an arm- and leg-developing station, along with separate press and squat racks, all for use with barbells and free-weight plates. The top of the squat rack comes off and can be replaced with a simple pulley system that also uses plates. With these pulleys the plates swing unguided and will wobble, which may be annoying to you. The bench folds up for storage and is removable for use as a slant board.

### ▶ DELUXE INCLINE PULLEY

#### Model 7743

SUNBEAM LEISURE PRODUCTS CO.
HOWARD BUSH DRIVE
NEOSHO, MO 64850
(417) 451-4550

PRICE: $107

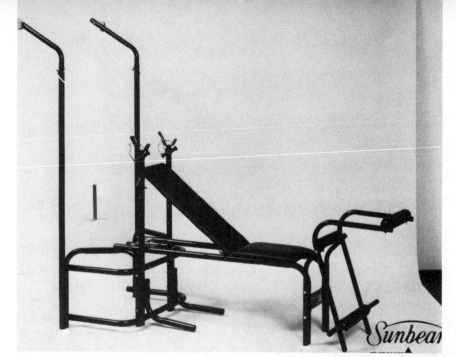

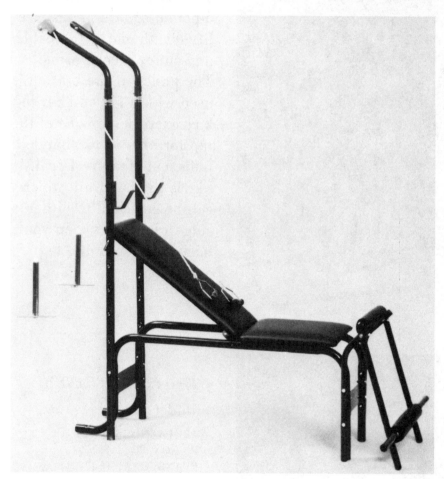

A less expensive, non-folding version of Sunbeam's Deluxe Foldaway. It has the simple pulley system/squat rack and a pair of hooks in place of a press rack. The leg-lift station can't be used for arm exercises as the more expensive version's can. The bench adjusts to five different inclines, but isn't removable.

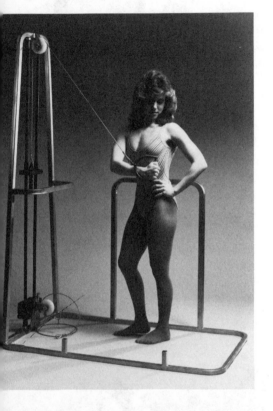

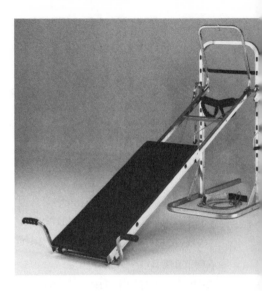

### ▶ *LEGACY*

LEGACY
1115 MADISON ST. NE
SUITE 131
SALEM, OR 97303
(503) 370-2886

PRICE: $285

The Legacy isn't for anyone who's looking to build big, bulging muscles. It's a toning and firming machine, and a good one at that. The weights (five 5-pound square plates) are lifted with one of two cable-and-pulley mechanisms. The pulley at the bottom is used with a leg cuff for leg kick exercise, the one at the top for one- or two-handed pulls. One feature I really like is the handrail, which can be switched to either side to help you keep your balance when doing leg exercises.

### ▶ *THE CONDITIONER*
### *Model 1265*

ARKLA INDUSTRIES
PO BOX 534
EVANSVILLE, IN 47704

PRICE: $299

The Arkla Family Gym series is very similar to the Total Gym machines, but is considerably cheaper. The Conditioner, Arkla's top-of-the-line model, costs the same as one of Total Gym's cheapest machines. The Conditioner has 12 angle settings, each of which increases resistance by 10 percent. There are two other models in the line: The Challenge ($229), with nine positions, and The Trimmer ($189), with three settings. All three machines come with instructions on how to use them for 106 different exercises. The benches on The Conditioner and The Challenge fold upwards so that they take up only about 48 square inches of floor space. The Trimmer doesn't fold.

### ▶ TOTAL GYM PRO
### *Model 42001*

WEST BEND CO.
WEST BEND, WI 53095

PRICE: $359
OPTIONS: SQUAT
STAND—$59.95
      WEIGHT BAR—$12.95
      CURL BENCH—$59.95

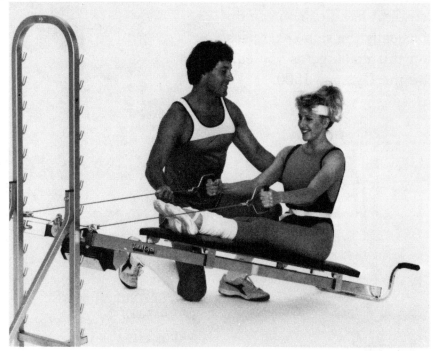

In this weight lifting system, your body supplies the resistance. The machine consists of a padded bench that moves along a steel frame on bearings. A pulley system connects the bench by cables to a set of padded metal handles. You sit or lie on the bench and pull the handles, moving yourself up and down the frame. To increase resistance, you hitch the bench onto a higher bracket, increasing the angle and the force required to move yourself. There are nine angle settings on this model.

Included also is a cuff to replace each handle so you can do leg pulls. Among the optional accessories is a curling accessory that mounts at the top of the bench. By supporting your elbows with it you can do biceps and forearm curls with one or both arms. Other options are a squat stand (really just a foot board) that permits you to approximate squats by sliding yourself up and down, and a weight bar that turns the machine into a traditional weight bench. All the Total Gym machines are freestanding but can be mounted to a wall with brackets.

### ► FAMILY FITNESS CENTER

BILLARD BARBELL CO.
208 CHESNUT ST.
READING, PA 19602
(215) 375-4333

PRICE: $360

The Family Fitness Center mounts on the wall and folds up for storage. Its twelve 10-pound plate weights are pin-loaded and are raised by pulleys. A leg cuff and handles are included, and the lift bar has both an angled and straight handle. You can do basically the same exercises on this machine as you can on the Gympac 1500.

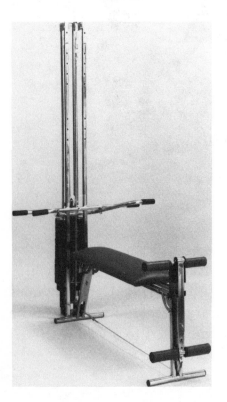

### ► OMNI-GYM

### Model 08612

JAYFRO
PO BOX 400
WATERFORD, CT 06385
(203) 447-3001

PRICE: $419

This budget multi-gym uses free weights and can accommodate two people at the same time. It has a squat rack, incline bench, leg-lift station and a weight pulley. The pulley system, which allows weights to swing free, isn't ideal.

The machine is made from galvanized steel tubing and has a plywood bench with 1 inch of urethane foam padding. The bench has a total weight capacity of 500 pounds when flat and 300 pounds when inclined.

STORAGE POSITION

### ▶ GYMPAC

#### Model 15-3300

DIVERSIFIED PRODUCTS
1935 EAST VIA ARADO
COMPTON, CA 90220
(213) 639-4720

PRICE: $455

Here's a basic wall-mounted pulley weight system designed primarily for women. It comes with long and short handlebars, a leg cuff and handgrips.

You can do about 30 exercises with the machine, among them lateral forward raises, two-armed curls, lateral pulls and leg raises. Standard equipment is five 11-pound weights, and you can order an additional 55 pounds.

### ▶ GYMPAC 1500

#### Model 15-05100

DIVERSIFIED PRODUCTS
1935 EAST VIA ARADO
COMPTON, CA 90220
(213) 639-4720

PRICE: $485

The Gympac 1500 is a first-rate home exercise unit at a reasonable price. You can usually find it for sale at large department stores at a discounted price.

The designers appear to have thought of all the important details when they came up with this machine. The little things, like built-in caster wheels for moving it around and plastic-coated weights for noise reduction, really add up.

The handlebar slides up and down on twin metal beams, so you're always in control of the load. The bar can be moved to six positions and has revolving handgrips so you can use it to do bench presses, squats, leg presses and chin-ups. Or you can remove the bars and attach hand and leg pulleys for leg pull-downs and arm pulls.

The bench, which is thickly padded and covered

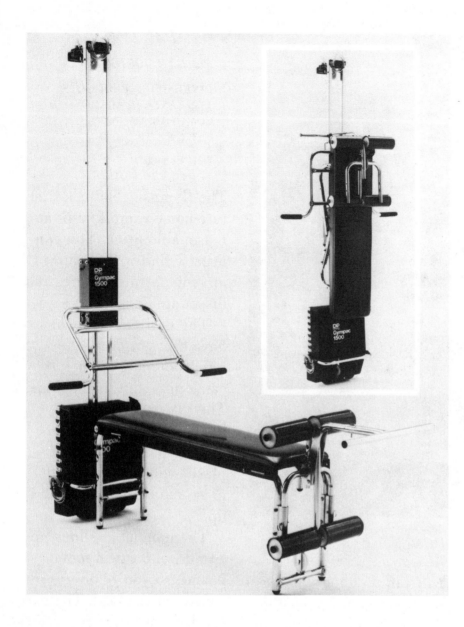

The rugged Brutus 1000 has a 10-position lifting bar, a single 100-pound weight stack in 10-pound increments, shock-absorbing bumper pads and ball-bearing pulleys. It can be mounted to the wall or stand by itself with an optional frame ($150).

▶ **BODYBAR 2000**

### Model 2000

MARCY FITNESS PRODUCTS
2801 W. MISSION RD.
ALHAMBRA, CA 91803
(213) 570-1222

PRICE: $500
OPTION: LEG PRESS—$45

Of all the multi-gyms in this price range that I tried, the Bodybar 2000 was the most pleasant to use. Its frame is

with candy-apple red metallic vinyl can be inclined for sit-ups (a foot strap is included) and there are leg-curl/extension bars that also hook into the pulley and weight stack for leg and arm curls.

The machine comes with eight 11-pound weights.

Another 88 pounds can be added if you need it.

▶ **BRUTUS 1000**

### Model 12-E1000

EXCEL
9935 BEVERLY BLVD.
PICO RIVERA, CA 90660
(800) 392-2258

PRICE: $498

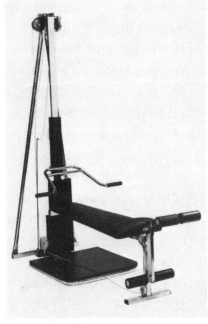

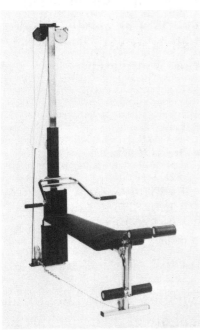

bench and leg station. It can be mounted on a wall, or you can buy a V-shaped frame ($196) to make it freestanding.

### ▶ *TOTAL GYM PRO PLUS AND COMPETITION PLUS*

#### *Models 42000 and 42002*

WEST BEND CO.
WEST BEND, WI 53095

PRICES: PRO PLUS—$499
            COMPETITION
            PLUS—$299

These are two other models in the Total Gym system.

The Pro Plus (left) comes with a squat stand (an option on other models) and side bars so you can add free weights to increase resistance above the level your body can supply. It has 11 angle settings.

The Competition Plus is $200 cheaper and has four fewer angle settings. It doesn't come with any accessories but accepts all the system's options except the free-weight bar.

very rigid and has the solid feel of a more expensive machine. This model has a single weight stack with high/low pulleys, an eight-position lifting arm and extra-thick pads on the

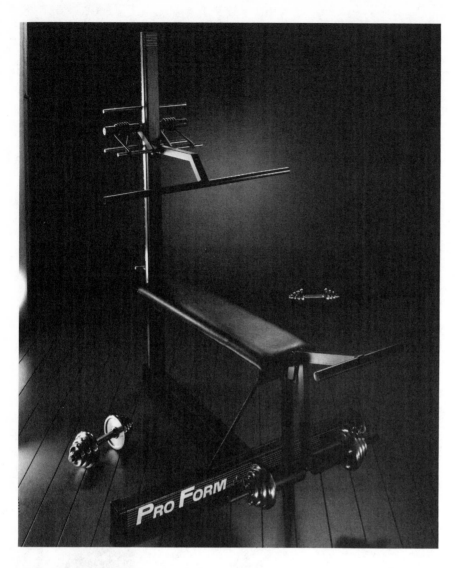

range of movement, with no "dead spots." You can perform lat and biceps curls, bent rowing exercises, bar pull-downs, dead lifts, bench presses, chin-ups and incline sit-ups. An optional leg-lift station uses conventional plate weights, and you can also add plates to the resistance bar.

The unit weighs 150 pounds and takes up only 4 square feet of floor space. It comes disassembled but can be put together in a half hour with the wrench that's provided.

### ▸ *PROFORM 2000*

#### *Model PPF200*

THE SHARPER IMAGE
PO BOX 26823
SAN FRANCISCO, CA 94126
(800) 344-4444

PRICE: $545
OPTION: LEG LIFT—$59

The ProForm multi-gym was obviously designed to take a bite out of Soloflex's big share of the market. The two machines look and work very much alike. But instead of the rubber discs that Soloflex uses for resistance, the ProForm has steel coil springs. You can add them one at a time, from the equivalent of 10 pounds up to as much as 170 pounds. There's also a padded bench where the Soloflex has bare wood.

The springs provide resistance over a wide

### ▸ *SOLOFLEX*

SOLOFLEX
HAWTHORN FARM
  INDUSTRIAL PARK
HILLSBORO, OR 97124
(800) 453-9000

PRICE: $565

Soloflex declined to provide a photo of their machine for this book, but if you've picked up a magazine in the past couple of years you probably know what it looks like. Reports are that the company sells thousands of units a month through their ads that feature large

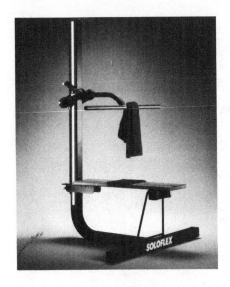

photos of well-muscled torsos.

The Soloflex is a handsome piece of equipment with its curved lines and matte-black finish with just a stripe of chrome. It's primarily a weight lifting machine but has the advantage of not using bulky plates. Resistance is supplied by thick rubber straps that slide over pins on a lever mechanism. The straps are capable of producing the same load as weights, but have a smoother and less clanky feel.

In its various configurations the Soloflex can be used as an incline bench, bench press, leg press and chin-up bar, as well as for biceps curls,

triceps push-downs, squats and triceps extensions.

As a competitor's ads gleefully point out, there's no way to do leg curls and extensions on a Soloflex. You'll have to buy a separate machine from another manufacturer if you want to do those exercises. I also think Soloflex should add some padding to their hard wooden bench.

▶ *THE LEAN MACHINE*

INERTIA DYNAMICS CORP.
3550 N. CENTRAL AVE.
PHOENIX, AZ 85012
(800) 821-7143

PRICE: $680 POSTPAID
OPTION: HEAVY-DUTY
      RESISTANCE
      PACKAGE—$59.95

The Lean Machine is another of the growing number of multi-gyms that use resistance devices instead of weights. In this case, the resistance is supplied via a cable pulley-and-cam arrangement with counterforce springs. As you exert pressure on one of its three bars, the cam equalizes the resistance through the entire movement. Resistance is adjustable by changing the

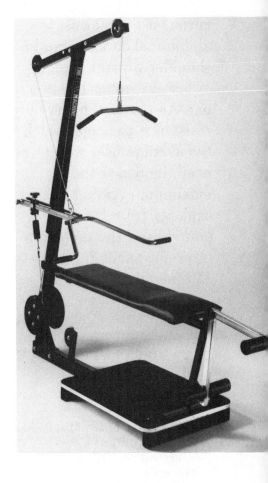

leverage on the main bar with a sliding scale, which shows measurements in pounds.

With the bench in place, you can do presses, pull-downs, inclined sit-ups and leg extensions and curls (the last station, an option on most of these machines, is standard on the Lean Machine). When the bench is removed there's a carpeted platform underneath to kneel or stand on when performing curls, lat pull-downs, abdominal curls, squats and shoulder presses using either the upper or lower bar. An optional heavy-duty resistance package, which the average user won't need, increases the maximum pressing station capacity from 200 to 280 pounds and the pull-down station capacity from 250 to 350 pounds.

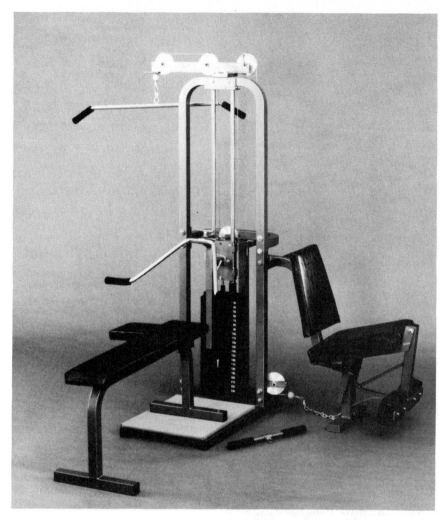

### ▶ *INTERNATIONAL BODY MACHINE*

#### *Model IBM*

EAST COAST BODY BUILDING
19 WARTBURG AVE.
COPIAGUE, NY 11726
(516) 842-1130

PRICE: $1,499

Although only one person at a time can train on this machine, there's no set-up required to change stations so you can move from one to the other as quickly as possible for aerobic benefit. There are high and low pulleys, a press station and a leg curl/extension bench connected to a 235-pound weight stack. (The first plate weighs 35 pounds, the rest are 10 pounds each.) This isn't the best-looking circuit trainer I've seen, but it is built to last.

### ▶ *FITNESS TRAINER II*

PARAMOUNT FITNESS
EQUIPMENT CO.
300 S. SANTA FE AVE.
LOS ANGELES, CA 90058
(800) 421-6242

PRICE: $1,695
OPTION: CHROME
                WEIGHTS—$195

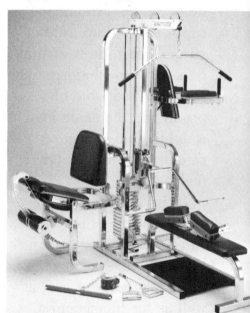

This multi-gym is a scaled-down version of the Fitness

Trainer (see page 000). The only major difference between the two models is that there's only one 170-pound stack on the Fitness Trainer II instead of the two the more expensive model has. The same options are available on both machines.

▶ *POWER PAK 300*

*Model PP3-100*

UNIVERSAL
PO BOX 1270
CEDAR RAPIDS, IA 52406
(319) 365-7561

PRICE: $1,875

The Power Pak 300 has the same quality construction and number of stations as the more expensive 400 series, but takes up less floor space. There's just one weight stack, connected to both the high and low pulleys, so only one person at a time can use the lifting stations. Also, the leg extension/curl bench must double as a seat for pressing. If you're usually the only one working out at a given time, I'd suggest saving the $670 and getting this model.

▶ *LIFESTYLER 9000*

*Model 150*

AMF AMERICAN
200 AMERICAN AVE.
JEFFERSON, IA 50129
(800) 247-3978

PRICE: $1,995

The Lifestyler 9000 has six separate exercise stations, (bench press, shoulder press, high pulley, high lat pulley, low pulley and abdominal board) yet takes up only 15 square feet of floor space.

The frame is made of very rigid 1½-by-3-inch rectangular steel tubing; the pulleys and cables are also steel. The removable bench has 2 inches of foam padding and is covered with tough vinyl. Standard equipment is a 150-pound weight stack, but you can order 200 pounds for an added $115.

### ▶ FITNESS TRAINER

PARAMOUNT FITNESS
EQUIPMENT CORP.
300 S. SANTA FE AVE.
LOS ANGELES, CA 90058
(800) 421-6242

PRICE: $2,195
OPTIONS: KNEE RAISE
        STATION—$195
        LEG EXTENSION
        STATION—$495
        CHROME
        WEIGHTS—$490

The Fitness Trainer is a professional-quality circuit trainer that lets you move from station to station within seconds for aerobic as well as muscular conditioning. It looks like sculpture with its curved lines and heavy nickel-chrome plated parts and it's definitely not something you can stick unobtrusively in a corner of the living room, even if you happen to have 60 square feet you're not using at the moment.

The standard model comes with a bench that's used for chest and shoulder presses, a high pulley for upper-back and triceps exercises, and a low pulley with handles and leg cuffs for curls, leg kicks and other pulls. There are two separate weight stacks both with pin selectors for quick changes. The press station has a total of 210 pounds; the pulleys, 105 pounds. Both are in 10-pound increments. The standard plates are black and are available in chrome.

With optional equipment you can add even more stations. The best, I think, are the leg-curl and leg-extension accessories. Rather than a bench, these use a space-saving chair (the seat flips up for standing leg curls). I also like the vertical leg raise option—it's the station with the padded back and armrests in the center of the photo above. You hop up onto it and support your weight with your lower arms while holding the handles, then you raise and lower your legs with your back straight. It's great exercise for the abdominal muscles.

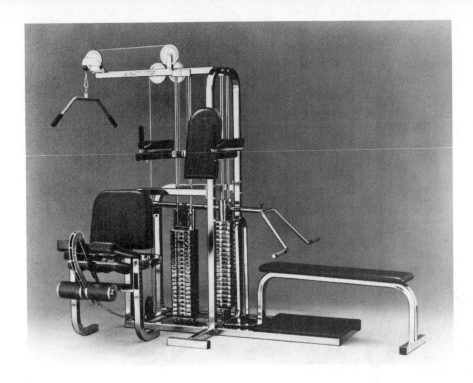

exercise. And utilizing the cylinders keeps the units compact and the lifting action smooth and quiet.

The Total Power has three cylinders, one for each of its stations (shoulder press, chest press and leg curl/extension). You can choose from six resistance and speed settings for all of the exercises. The meter panel has gauges that approximate the number of pounds you're moving.

► **TOTAL POWER**

*Model 311*

HYDRA-FITNESS
PO BOX 599
BELTON, TX 76513
(800) 433-3111

PRICE: $2,455

The Hydra-Fitness line of machines uses hydraulic cylinders, rather than weights, for resistance. You get resistance when you push or pull the handles, so you can work opposing sets of muscles in the same

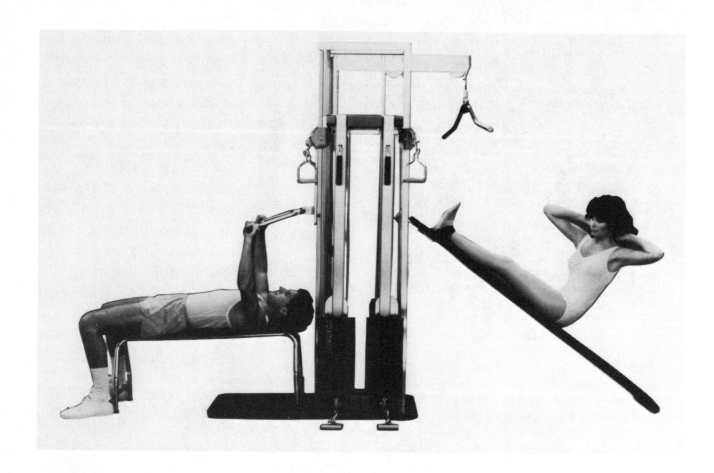

### ▶ FAMILY FITNESS CENTER

#### Model 1399

MARCY FITNESS PRODUCTS
2801 W. MISSION RD.
ALHAMBRA, CA 91803
(213) 570-1222

PRICE: $2,500

Marcy equipment has gained quite a following recently (Clint Eastwood and Ronald Reagan among them). Their weight machines are well built and look good, and you can often find them substantially discounted.

The Family Fitness Center is their best multi-gym. It comes with high and low pulleys, a pull-down bar, press station with an eight-position arm and incline bench. The only feature not included that I might miss is a leg curl station. There are two weight stacks, 220 and 180 pounds, so more than one person can exercise on the multi-gym at the same time.

### ▶ POWER PAK 400

#### Model PP4-100

UNIVERSAL
PO BOX 1270
CEDAR RAPIDS, IA 52406
(319) 365-7561

PRICE: $2,595
OPTIONS: LEG PRESS—$70
LEG SQUAT—$160
80-POUND WEIGHT
ADD-ON—$185

Universal's name has become synonymous with circuit training. This is their top-drawer home unit, built to the same specifications as the machines they make for

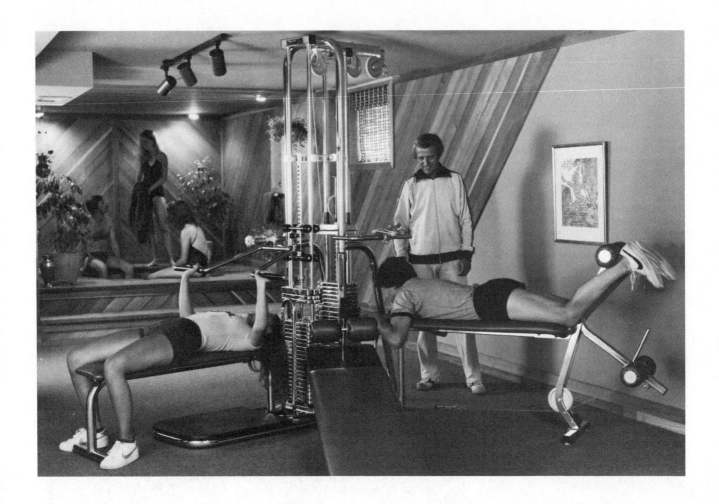

health clubs. The 2-inch-diameter heavy tubing is nickel-chrome plated, and all cables are 2,000-pound-test with self-aligning nylon bushings.

The basic unit shown here has six stations: a high and low pulley, chest/shoulder press, an adjustable abdominal board and a leg extension/curl attachment that connects with the low pulley. There are two standard weight stacks, so that two can work out on the machine at the same time—115 pounds for the pulleys, 100 pounds for the press station. If you want chromed weights like the ones on this model, instead of the standard black, they'll set you back an outrageous $760! Don't ask me why.

▶ *VERSA-CLIMBER*
*Model CL108*

HEART RATE, INC.
3001 REDHILL AVE.
COSTA MESA, CA 92626
(714) 850-9716

PRICE: $2,795

Climbing is good exercise, but hard to get in a home gym. This isn't exactly a multi-gym, but it combines both aerobic and resistance exercises. The Versa-Climber can give you all the benefits of vertical climbing while keeping you less than 2 feet off the ground, that is, if you can afford the steep price.

The machine is 8 feet tall and set at a 75-degree angle. To use it you grab one of its three sets of hand grips and slip your feet into the covered pedals. Then you step down on the highest pedal while pulling down on the corresponding grip. That makes the pedal and grip on the other side move upward. Up and down resistance, as well as stroke force, length and rate are adjustable.

For lower body exercise alone, you can hold onto a set of stationary grips and just work the pedals. Or, you can stand off the pedals and just do arm pulls. A three-screen monitor at eye level displays time, total distance and number of strokes.

In a 6-week study at Chapman College in Orange, California, using the Versa-Climber for a total of eighteen 20-minute sessions body fat was found to decrease by an average of 4.5 percent while increasing aerobic fitness in the 24 test subjects.

# ▶ GYM ON A WALL

RODALE PRESS
33 E. MINOR ST.
EMMAUS, PA 18049
(215) 967-5171

PRICE: PLANS—$14.95

If you're handy with tools and have a home workshop, you can build this multi-gym for about $250. It has six stations including pulley weights, chin-up bar, slant board and a sliding bench and pulley system that lets you use your own weight for resistance. Everything folds up and fits inside the wall-mounted cabinet. The book comes with complete blueprints, building instructions and an exercise manual.

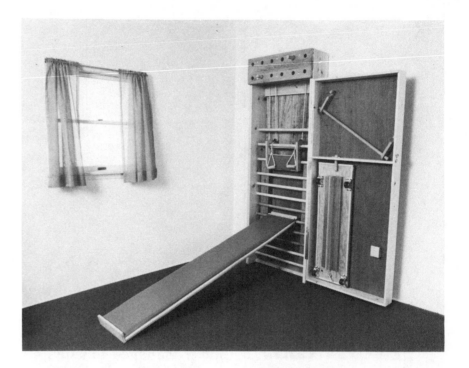

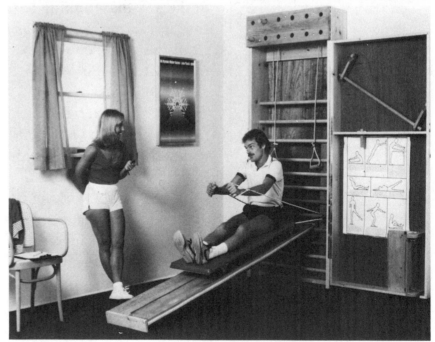

# ROWING MACHINES

Rowing may be one of the most underrated exercises around. Although it has never managed to catch on in the way that running has, rowing can get you just as fit in the same amount of time, but with far less chance of injury.

As aerobic exercise, rowing is nothing short of great. By starting with only four 15-minute sessions a week and slowly working up to 35-minute workouts, you can significantly increase the amount of oxygen your body takes in and processes in just two months. When you're really pushing, you'll be taking in twice the volume of air of an unconditioned person.

At 20 strokes per minute, an hour of rowing burns up 540 calories. If you want to think of it another way, that's about one banana split or one and a half cheeseburgers.

Rowing also builds stamina, flexibility and endurance, as well as putting all the major muscle areas of your body to work. Yet because the action is mostly pushing and pulling, there's very little trauma to your joints. Other than an occasional minor back strain, it's almost impossible to hurt yourself rowing indoors. That's why some doctors recommend it for patients with arthritis and other orthopedic ailments.

College sculling teams and sport rowers often use indoor machines to keep in shape during the winter. The equipment simulates the movement and action of real rowing almost perfectly with hydraulics or tension devices simulating the resistance of the water. Most rowing machines even have sliding seats like real sculls so that the power of the stroke can be increased by leg pushes.

Lots of people who never go near the water have also discovered mechanical rowers. In the past few years the machines have become one of the top five types of equipment found in home gyms. There are scores of models on the market and sadly, more than a few are real bummers. I've seen brands that were made from metal tubing no more rugged than the kind used on lawn furniture and tried some that had seats so jittery I almost got seasick. Other problems were ''oars'' that didn't work smoothly and were hard to adjust, and machines so light they jumped several inches with each stroke.

There are many good rowing machines out there, and often they don't cost a lot more than the bad ones. Quality brands usually have

padded or contoured seats that slide smoothly on rollers and ball bearings. The seat should move a good distance—as much as 27 inches—so even tall people can stretch their legs. The foot pads ought to adjust to a number of angles or at the very least have a bar or Velcro strap to keep your feet in place.

Handles, or oars, come in two basic variations. The simplest are one-piece curved metal tubing with a grip on the end. These move only forward and backward. Expensive machines sometimes have pivoting arms that also allow circular movement while you row. Which type is better is a matter of preference.

In any case, make sure the oars on the rowing

machine you select are made of sturdy tubing so they won't bend under the force of the exercises. And don't even think about buying a machine that doesn't have adjustable resistance. Without this feature, you'll outgrow the machine in a matter of weeks.

▶ *HOME ROWER*
*Model TR-100*

MCA SPORTS
689 FIFTH AVE.
NEW YORK, NY 10022
(800) 423-6637

PRICE: $120

If you're looking for a rower to use once in a while for a change of pace, the price is right on this one. It has a single T-bar rowing arm, adjustable foot straps and a soft seat that rides on

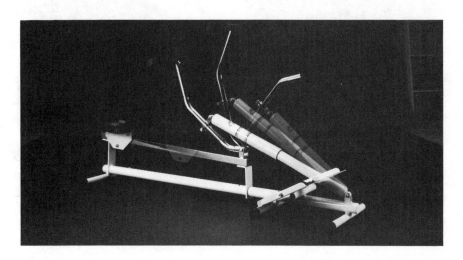

one rail. If rowing will be your main exercise, I'd suggest investing in a more expensive twin-oar model.

### ▶ *JAGUAR 2000*

#### *Model J2000*

AMF WHITELY
29 ESSEX ST.
MAYWOOD, NJ 07607
(201) 843-3210

PRICE: $130

The Jaguar 2000 looks like a stationary bike but is actually a type of indoor rower. Its one-piece pivoting exercise bar has footrests on the bottom and hand grips on the top. The movement is a rowing motion that uses feet and hands. Resistance is supplied by five steel springs and can be adjusted by adding or removing one or more of them. This design is functional, but noisier than most hydraulic rowing machines.

### ▶ *HYDRAULIC ROWER*

#### *Model RM-6*

VITAMASTER INDUSTRIES
455 SMITH ST.
BROOKLYN, NY 11231
(212) 858-0505

PRICE: $155

This very basic rower has few amenities. There are no footrests or straps, just a metal bar to push against. The relatively hard seat slides on round metal tubes rather than a single beam. The frame is welded, but the crosspieces and oar mechanisms are bolted on. There are three resistance settings: light, medium and heavy.

### ▶ *DELUXE ROWER*

#### *Model RM-907*

VITAMASTER INDUSTRIES
455 SMITH ST.
BROOKLYN, NY 11231
(212) 858-0505

PRICE: $170

Features include a sloping center slide beam, well-padded seat and one-piece steel footrest with adjustable straps. The independent chrome rowing arms have unlimited resistance settings which

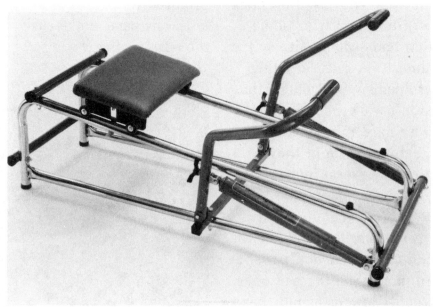

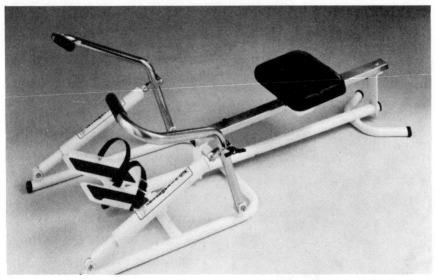

which can soil light-colored carpets.

▶ *TUNTURI HOME ROWER*

*Model ATHR*

AMEREC
BOX 3825
BELLEVUE, WA 98009
(800) 643-1000

PRICE: $300

Although the Home Rower is Amerec's bottom-of-the-line model, it's well manufactured and has padded footrests, a smooth-gliding seat and infinite resistance settings. It's hampered by having only a single rowing arm with a handlebar for both hands. I think rowing is more

are changed by sliding the shock absorber clamp up and down the lower length of the oars.

▶ *ROWTEC*

*Model 515*

WALTON MANUFACTURING CO.
106 REGAL ROW
DALLAS, TX 75247
(214) 637-2500

PRICE: $199

The jointed arms of the Rowtec rotate to simulate the dipping action of actual rowing. Adjustable resistance is supplied by a ratchet and disc brake mechanism at the joint, but there is tension only on the pull stroke. The individual footrests are on a sliding bar so you can customize

the machine to your height. By keeping your feet under the straps and moving the oars out of the way the Rowtec can be used as a sit-up bench. By the way, the manufacturer warns that wear on the disc brake pads produces a dark dust

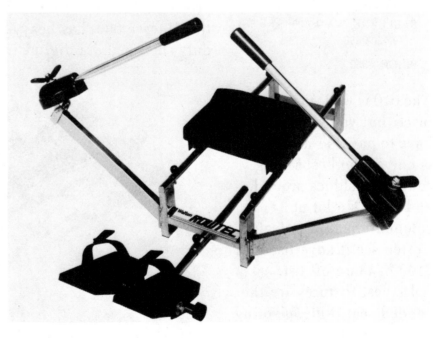

enjoyable and less boring when you can move both hands independently.

### ▶ AMEREC 610

**Model A610**

AMEREC
PO BOX 3825
BELLEVUE, WA 98009
(800) 426-0858

PRICE: $350

The 610 is well worth its list price, but you should never have to pay that much. This is one of the best-selling rowing machines around, and there's a lot of competition among dealers. I often see it advertised for $100 or more off list.

Its best features are the padded seat, wide, pivoting foot pedals and independent stainless-steel oars. The lightweight frame is made of aluminum and the whole machine can be wall-mounted and used for doing arm curls, dead lifts and biceps and triceps presses. A deluxe version, the Amerec 660, has heavy-duty shocks and a digital stroke counter. It lists for $550.

### ▶ AVITA 950

M&R INDUSTRIES
9215 151ST AVE. NE
REDMOND, WA 98052
(206) 885-1010

PRICE: $350

The 950 is a very smooth, precision rower. Its twin resistance cylinders are gas-assisted to eliminate dead spots, and the oars are mounted on sealed ball bearings that stay tight and don't need maintenance. The parts are welded together instead of bolted, so the frame has a solid, rigid feel. (It's guaranteed for five years.) The seat is a beauty—3½ inches of padding and quiet when it moves. There's a 60-minute timer but no stroke counter.

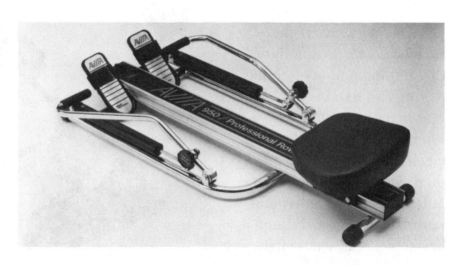

### ▶ TUNTURI ROWING MACHINE

**Model ATRM**

AMEREC
PO BOX 3825
BELLEVUE, WA 98009
(800) 643-1000

PRICE: $350

For an extra $50, this seems like a better buy than the Tunturi Home Rower. It has dual rowing arms that can be adjusted separately. There are four primary resistance settings, but you can fine-tune it to your own preferred level anywhere between the click stops.

### ▶ PROFORM 935

**Model PPF935**

THE SHARPER IMAGE
PO BOX 26823
SAN FRANCISCO, CA 94126
(800) 344-4444

PRICE: $365.50 POSTPAID

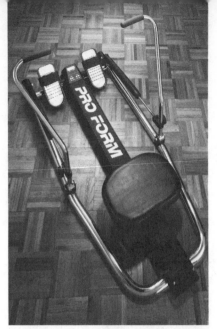

There are lots of nice features on the Proform 935. It utilizes smooth, gas-pressurized shocks for resistance rather than hydraulic cylinders. The handles have soft foam grips and ball bearings at the joints. Between the adjustable, independent footrests is an electronic console which has a four-tone audible metronome to act as a built-in coxswain, as well as a timer and photoelectric stroke counter. A good buy at a reasonable price.

### ▶ DELUXE ROWING MACHINE

**Model FSRM-11**

JAYFRO
PO BOX 400
WATERFORD, CT 06385
(203) 447-3001

PRICE: $369

The frame is chrome-dipped welded steel and has rubber mounts to protect your floors. Cast aluminum footrests pivot and have nylon web straps. The contoured seat is raised about 12 inches from the floor. That's higher than many rowing machines and may be more comfortable for some people.

### ▶ *CONCEPT II*

CONCEPT II INC.
RFD 2, BOX 6410
MORRISVILLE, VT 05661

PRICE: $595

The Concept II has caused quite a stir in the world of rowing machines. Enthusiasts are even organizing indoor "regattas" using the device. The competitors line up their machines and see who can row a predetermined distance in the fastest time. More than 500 people participated in one of these races.

You've got to admit it's different. There's nothing on the machine that even *looks* like a set of oars. Instead there's a handle connected to a drive chain which is wrapped around the hub of a bicycle wheel with little plastic fins on it. The spinning of the flywheel creates momentum for smooth action, and the fins act as a drag mechanism. The hub has two gear settings to change resistance levels.

You start the stroke with the seat forward—knees bent and arms extended. Then you kick back with your feet, keeping your arms straight. Finally, when your legs are fully extended, you bend your arms pulling the handle toward your abdomen and then return to the forward position. A speedometer and odometer help you monitor your progress.

The fluid action of the chain and flywheel probably come closer to recreating the actual feeling of rowing than any other type of machine can. The only real drawbacks to the Concept II are that you can't exercise your arms independently because of the single handle and that at 100 inches long, it takes up considerably more space than ordinary rowing machines.

### ▶ *EXEROW*

BATTLE CREEK EQUIPMENT CO.
307 WEST JACKSON ST.
BATTLE CREEK, MI 49017
(800) 253-0854

PRICE: $789

The Exerow is a single-arm, upright rowing machine that supplies resistance on both the push and pull strokes. Pushing the adjustable handle away from you also moves the

seat back and down to stretch you. Pulling the handle brings the seat up again. By grabbing it underhanded you can do a modified curling exercise.

Resistance comes from a single hydraulic cylinder that has three tension settings: light, medium and heavy. The cylinder is designed to last through at least 2 million repetitions, and the entire bike has a one-year guarantee that covers parts and labor.

# TREADMILLS

Jogging has to get a lot of credit for getting the fitness movement in this country on its feet. Jogging, or running if you prefer that interchangeable term, seemingly came out of nowhere in the mid-70s. As more and more people saw friends and neighbors getting thin and fit through running, they donned sweats and shoes themselves and hit the road. By the time the pastime hit its stride a few years later, more than 30 million Americans were taking part; that number divides about equally between men and women. Nowadays you can't travel anywhere without seeing joggers lining the streets and parkways. The sales of running shoes alone have now hit the $1 billion-a-year mark.

For the most part, the rise of running has been a very positive phenomenon. Using your legs to propel your body over several miles of road is incredibly good aerobic exercise. It vastly increases the amount of oxygen the lungs take in and process, and it trains the heart to be much more efficient. In addition to building stamina, agility and endurance, most avid runners report that the activity produces a natural, calming high, the result of exercise-stimulated chemicals in the brain.

The reason so many runners get thin is that jogging is a real calorie burner. Even a beginner who alternately runs and walks can use up 10 calories a minute in the process.

In spite of its obvious benefits, quite a lot of medical controversy has surrounded jogging in recent years. Most of the questions have to do with the frequent injuries runners are prone to. It's true that few people who have been running any distance for a long time have escaped without some physical complaints. They range from simple shin splints and pulled muscles to broken bones, compressed vertabrae, knee and joint pain and even chronic diarrhea.

Too many of these problems are the result of overdoing it. Joggers who train more than three times a week for a half-hour per session have a significantly higher rate of injury. But besides that, physical ailments may be due to the nature of the beast. Running puts an average of five times more pressure than normal on the ankles, feet and legs. Considering that your feet smack the ground as many as 700 times a mile when running, some injuries are unavoidable. Jogging is a traumatic form of exercise; it's as simple as that.

Still, there are some jogging injuries that fall more into the class of accidents: slips on icy streets, car accidents, bites from unfriendly dogs. One friend of mine broke an ankle in an encounter with an unseen gopher hole while (foolishly) running across a farmer's field.

Jogging safely indoors, on a treadmill, is one way to avoid these accidents. While few diehard runners are willing to give up the open road entirely for the relative protection of indoor exercise, treadmills are useful for keeping up a training schedule when the weather's not cooperating. For those people who have never taken up running or who have given it up because of the hassles, treadmills provide a means to take part in the sport.

All treadmills are basically alike in that they have a flat, flexible running surface which moves over wooden, plastic or metal rollers. However, the similarities between motorized and manual treadmills end right about there.

On a manual model, you supply the energy that keeps the running surface moving around the rollers. On motorized versions the treadmill moves electrically at the speed you select beforehand.

Both types have their advantages and disadvantages. I've heard manual treadmills criticized for a number of reasons, some legitimate and others not. For example, it's been said that it's uncomfortable to use them barefooted. True, but you shouldn't be running without the padding and protection of shoes in the first place. Others say that using them takes some practice and it's easier to lose your balance on one. Again, partly true. All good treadmills come with handrails. As long as they're sturdy and you hang on, there's no reason to fall even if you slip. And they do take some getting used to, but not so much that the technique can't be mastered in a day. Manual treadmills are noisier than motorized ones, but they're also much cheaper and easier to maintain.

An electric treadmill is a luxury, probably worth the price if you can afford it. While a decent manual model can be had for $300, motorized versions start at $1,000, and some can set you back by the price of a Toyota station wagon.

An electric treadmill is the only motorized exercise device I can recommend. That's because the motor isn't making the exercise any easier for you, it's just carrying the running surface in the opposite direction you're headed. To use this device, all you do is start the motor and set the tread at the desired speed. Then you step (carefully) on, using the handrails, and start running.

A big advantage of having an electric model is that you can gradually increase the speed of the tread to pace yourself for harder running. On most you can also increase the angle of the surface to simulate hills. Other features to look for are handrails on the front and side, a built-in timer and an easy-to-reach on/off switch.

Other than the price, there are few drawbacks to electric treadmills. If something goes haywire, you'll probably have to have it repaired, which can be troublesome. And because of their size, motorized models don't usually fold up for storage like some manual ones. If space is a concern, shop for a treadmill that has retractable casters and hope you have a closet big enough to store the machine in.

Since treadmill running is easier in some ways than jogging outdoors, there may be more temptation to push yourself further than you ought to. Don't forget that even though the running surface is softer than pavement, running is running and there's always some trauma to the legs. Set reasonable goals for yourself, and don't run long distances more than three times a week. There's little gain in overtraining and a much higher risk you'll hurt yourself.

▶ *AEROBIC WALKER*
*Model 650*

WALTON MANUFACTURING CO.
106 REGAL ROW
DALLAS, TX 75247
(214) 637-2500

PRICE: $239

This short (49 inches) manual treadmill doesn't provide enough surface for running, but can be used for fast walking exercises. The 14-inch-wide plastic tread moves on 21 rollers housed in a welded steel frame. It has a front rail only with an odometer/speedometer. There's probably no reason to buy a limited-use treadmill like this unless you have a health problem that prevents running.

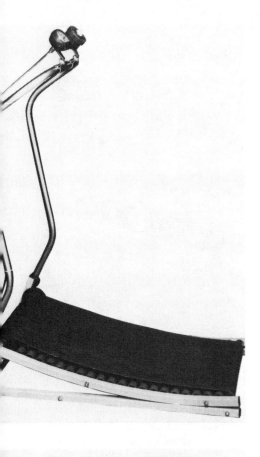

### ▶ TREADMASTER
### Model J-16RS

VITAMASTER INDUSTRIES
455 SMITH ST.
BROOKLYN, NY 11231
(212) 858-0505

PRICE: $280

You won't find any treadmills less expensive than this one. The mat is made of nylon-reinforced vinyl and slides over hardwood rollers. A 4-pound flywheel on the front roller helps to smooth out the tread action. Incline is adjustable, but not tread resistance. Give this one a long try before deciding to buy. You may want to opt for a more expensive model with additional features such as Vitamaster's Pro-7000.

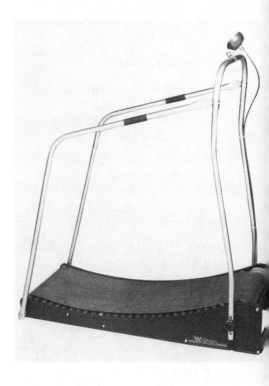

### ▶ JOGACISER
### Model 660

WALTON MANUFACTURING CO.
106 REGAL ROW
DALLAS, TX 75247
(214) 637-2500

PRICE: $299

This is a good manual treadmill with curved, steel-roller running track, sturdy front and side rails and caster wheels for moving. The rails fold down, and the whole unit can be tipped up on its feet end for storage. The speedometer has a top speed of 6 mph.

### ▶ INSIDE LANE

### *Model J-4800*

EXERCYCLE CORP.
667 PROVIDENCE ST.
WOONSOCKET, RI 02895
(401) 331-0113

PRICE: $669
OPTIONS: SIDE RAILS—$71
         60-MINUTE
         TIMER—$20

What I like best about this 48-inch-long manual treadmill is the telescoping front rail that comes with dropped handgrips and a safety belt you can wear to help you keep your balance. The tread is made of cleated rubber for sure footing. The rollers are made of heavy-gauge steel and are attached to a welded frame.

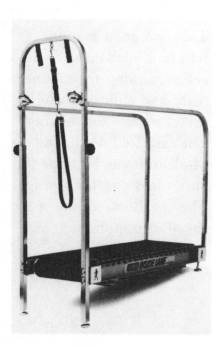

The otherwise thoughtful design of this treadmill is marred by the fact that the belt tension is pre-set at the factory and can't be changed. The only way to progressively increase your workouts is to raise the incline.

### ▶ PACESETTER

### *Model 2001*

MARCY FITNESS PRODUCTS
2801 W. MISSION RD.
ALHAMBRA, CA 91803
(213) 570-1222

PRICE: $675

The running bed on this 49-inch treadmill has a deep dip in the middle to keep your feet from slipping off the back, a common problem with manual joggers. There are three incline settings but, surprisingly, no resistance adjustment. This seems like a major flaw in a machine as expensive as the Pacesetter.

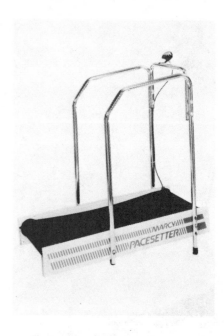

### ▶ PRO-7000

### *Model J-7000*

VITAMASTER INDUSTRIES
455 SMITH ST.
BROOKLYN, NY 11231
(212) 858-0505

PRICE: $680

The Pro-7000 is one of the better manual treadmills around, and the price reflects the extra quality. One excellent feature is the flat running surface. There are only two rollers, at the front and rear, so you don't get that uneasy feeling of running on rolling pins as you do on some less expensive models. The track itself is made of a slightly sticky plastic that does a good job of gripping

your shoe soles. There are three incline levels to choose from, adjustable by pulling out two pins and raising the legs. The tension control is located right at your fingertips, next to the LED display that continuously reads out your time, distance and speed.

I found that my feet had a tendency to slip off the back of the treadmill when the incline was in the highest setting. Holding onto the front rail and leaning slightly forward as I ran seemed to alleviate the problem.

### ▶ AVITA 300

M&R INDUSTRIES
9215 151ST AVE. NE
REDMOND, WA 98052
(206) 885-1010

PRICE: $699

With a running tread 40 inches long and 16 inches wide, the Avita 300 is smaller than many treadmills. That's fine if you want to save space, but could be a problem for taller people. It's a manual treadmill that runs on aluminum rollers and has a ½–25 mph governed speed range. The incline is variable from 2 to 14 percent grades. There's an odometer that measures to $\frac{1}{100}$th of a mile, but it's mounted down near the tread where it may be hard for some people to read it.

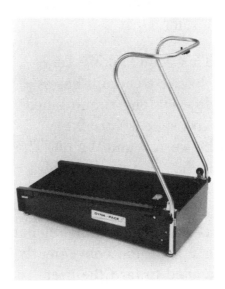

### ▶ TUNTURI JOGGING MACHINE
### *Model ATJM*

AMEREC
PO BOX 3825
BELLEVUE, WA 98009
(800) 426-0858

PRICE: $850

A good, moderately-priced manual treadmill, the Finnish-made Tunturi Jogging Machine features two counterbalanced flywheels up front for momentum and a tracking

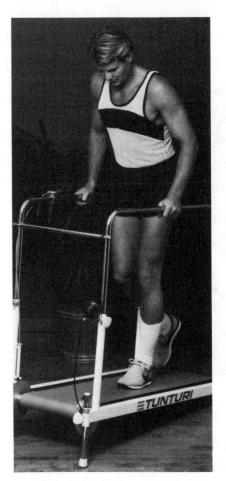

adjustment to keep the running mat from slipping off-center. It's 55-inches long, allowing a 39½-inch running stride. A resistance adjustment is located within convenient reach on the right handrail.

### ▶ *TREDEX MANUAL*

#### *Model 2902*

UNIVERSAL FITNESS
PRODUCTS
20 TERMINAL DRIVE
PLAINVIEW, NY 11803
(516) 349-8600

PRICE: $1,360

This high-quality manual treadmill is made entirely of steel, including the tread roller. I like the screw-type incline adjustment that raises the track up to a 15 percent grade. I'm also impressed by the design of the handrail, which angles back almost to the middle of the track and can be used as either a front or side support. But I've got to admit I was shocked by the price. You may not need a manual treadmill that can take the kind of abuse that this one will.

### ▶ *OMNI ELECTRO RUN*

#### *Model 1553*

MACLEVY PRODUCTS CORP.
43-23 91ST PLACE,
ELMHURST, NY 11373
(800) 221-0277

PRICE: $1,395

This good-looking 1-hp electric treadmill has a 4½-foot-long running bed with speeds variable between 0 and 9 mph. The incline is not adjustable. Tall people may find the side rails too low to be useful. The front handlebar is higher and conveniently angled toward the user.

### ▶ *STRIDE-SETTER*

#### *Model 699*

WALTON MANUFACTURING CO.
106 REGAL ROW
DALLAS, TX 75247
(214) 637-2500

PRICE: $1,495

Motorized treadmills aren't cheap, but this one offers lots of features for the money: a 7-mph top speed, an on/off switch that can be locked with a key, heavy-duty side rails with hand grips, an electric speedometer and 30-minute timer that shuts the machine off at a pre-set time, and caster wheels for easy moving. The steel-roller running bed is

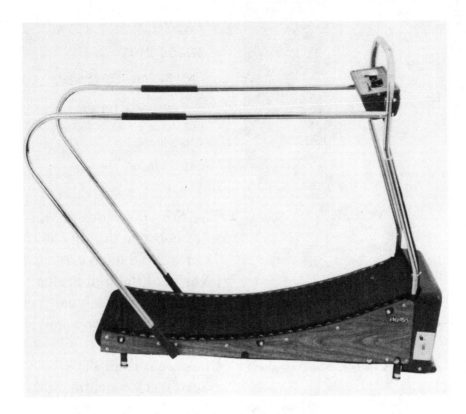

automatically. The result is a smooth, steady run and less chance of injury from overexertion.

The speed/pace settings are adjustable up to 12 mph using a lever that's always within easy reach. Incline can be varied between 3 and 13 degrees. (Running one mile at a 7-degree angle is equal in effort to doing 2½ miles on a flat surface.) The dial console near the front of the tread has a speedometer, odometer and a 60-minute timer with buzzer.

curved, which supposedly reduces some of the pounding action of running and allows for a more natural stride. The Stride-Setter is available with a built-in digital exercise and pulse-rate monitor for an extra $174.

### ▶ THE WORLD CLASS AEROBIC TRAINER

SPORTECH, INC.
PO BOX 99101
CLEVELAND, OH 44199
(800) 221-1258

PRICE: $1,995

Several Olympic marathoners use this treadmill to train. The Aerobic Trainer looks like it ought to be a motorized treadmill, but it's not. Neither is it a free-spinning manual. This is an isokinetic device which has a built-in governor that you set for the maximum speed you want to run. You power the tread with your feet and legs, but no matter how hard you push it won't go faster than the pre-set speed. Instead, the more you push the more resistance there will be against your stride. As you tire and run less hard, the resistance decreases

► *TREDEX*
### *Model 2905*

UNIVERSAL FITNESS
PRODUCTS
20 TERMINAL DRIVE
PLAINVIEW, NY 11803
(516) 349-8600

PRICE: $3,790

The *Star Wars* design and solid construction of the Tredex 2905 have made it a favorite of the well-heeled. I even spot it occasionally in the background of a movie or television show. Underneath the sleek exterior is a versatile and feature-laden 240-volt electric treadmill.

The direct-drive 1½-hp DC motor is electronically controlled and needs no transmission. It moves the stretch-resistant plastic tread at speeds variable up to 12½ mph, although I don't know many runners who could keep that speed up for long.

Electrodes in a belt that wraps around your chest pick up your heart rate and flash it to a digital display on the control panel, which also shows speed, distance and time measurements. The on/off and speed-setting controls are the

pressure-sensitive membrane type.

One feature I particularly like is that the safety handles in the front double as an emergency shut-off when you push them downward. There aren't any side rails, however, so you've got to be careful and pay attention to your running.

A cheaper model, the 2904, sells for $3,210. The only major differences are a motor ½ HP less powerful and a top speed of 8 mph, more than speedy enough for most people.

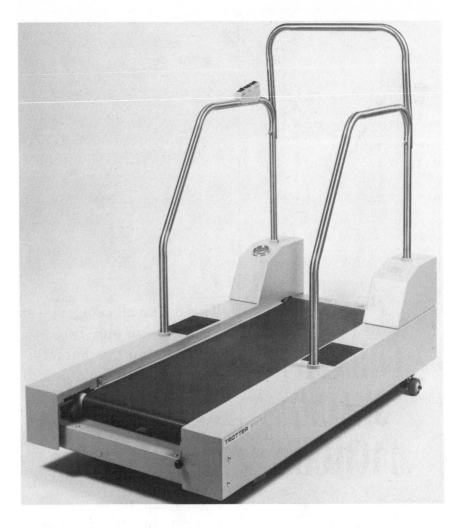

### ▶ *TROTTER 3100E*

TROTTER TREADMILLS, INC.
24 HOPEDALE ST.
HOPEDALE, MA 01747
(617) 473-0600

PRICE: $4,495
OPTION: SPECIAL
        COLOR—$150

The Trotter 3100E may lack the streamlined shape of some of the other treadmills, but that's just an indication that this is a no-nonsense machine built to take a lot of abuse. Trotter treadmills are probably used by more commercial health clubs than any other brand. With the flip of a switch its 1½-hp electric motor will move the running surface from a leisurely 1 mph to a more strenuous 12 mph (the pace for running a 5-minute mile). There's also an elevation adjustment for a 0 to 25 percent grade. An emergency shut-off switch will stop the tread in less than one second.

The chassis is constructed of 12-gauge steel finished with polyurethane. It comes in basic beige but you can order other colors if you give the company six weeks notice and $150.

The 3100E comes with retractable casters so you can move it around fairly easily, but at more than 5 feet long and 2½ feet wide, it's not exactly a piece of equipment that can be slipped into a closet when it's not being used.

# CROSS-COUNTRY SKIING MACHINES

This is a small category—so far there are only two machines on the market—but one worth looking into. As a sport, cross-country skiing has about 3 million followers in the United States. Dr. Kenneth Cooper, one of the foremost fitness experts in the country, has rated it the best kind of aerobic exercise, better for your heart and lungs than swimming, running or bicycling. And a Finnish study of 396 endurance skiers showed that they lived an average of 2.8 years longer than the general male population.

Gliding on skis may *look* easy, but actually the back and forth motion against resistance gives the legs a strenuous workout. At the same time, it's gentle on the bones and joints, which is why many former runners who sustained knee injuries pursuing that activity have taken up cross-country skiing and bought indoor machines. Moreover, the poling action of skiing involves lots of muscles in the arms, shoulders and upper body and builds strength there that running doesn't.

Ed Pauls developed the first cross-country skiing machine, the NordicTrack, in 1975 after spending one too many winter evenings jogging along icy roads when the skiing conditions weren't right. "I thought there was no reason why I couldn't build an exerciser to duplicate cross-country skiing motions," he says.

"Then I could train indoors and never miss a session because of outdoor conditions."

Pauls's machine and its competitor, the Fitness Master XC-1, do a fairly accurate job of simulating the feel and exertion of the real thing. Both have sliding foot pieces and a mechanism to simulate poling action. Each also has variable-resistance settings to help you train for the tough hills outdoors.

Be forewarned, though, that even six months of hard training on a skiing machine can't fully prepare you for a 10-degrees-below-zero day over *real* hills covered with a foot of new snow. Cross-country skiing is one of the safest of all sports, but the injuries that do occur, usually strained backs or tendinitis, are most often the result of overdoing it the first day out. Go slowly at first and stick to the flatlands.

Of course, nothing says you ever have to go near a snowy field to benefit from one of these devices. For total-body fitness with a dash of fun, they're worth a serious look from anyone

putting together a home gym.

▶ *NORDICTRACK*

### *Model 505*

PSI
124 COLUMBIA COURT
CHASKA, MN 55318
(800)328-5888

PRICE: $470
OPTION: PULSE METER—$108

This is the original and best-known cross-country ski machine. Your feet slide into toe cups attached to ¾-inch red oak "skis" that run on rollers attached to a flywheel. Resistance, which is only supplied on the backward push, comes from

an adjustable brake on the flywheel.

To control your balance while exercising you must lean forward against a hip-level padded support. Some users might find this awkward. Instead of ski poles, you have a long cord with handles on each end to move back and forth as you ski. It, too, has a brake for variable resistance. The arm and leg movements are independent, and the stroke length isn't pre-set, so you can adapt it to your own height and style. By removing two pins, the NordicTrack can be folded to 15 by 17 inches.

## ▶ FITNESS MASTER
### Model XC-1

FITNESS MASTER, INC.
12 HAVERHILL
JOHNATHAN, MN 55318
(800)328-8995

PRICE: $579

It's no coincidence that both brands of cross-country ski machines come from the same part of Minnesota. The Fitness Master was designed by a former NordicTrack executive who claims to have a better idea. In any case, he's come up with a machine that's quite different from its competitor's. Instead of a hip pad to balance you, there are sturdy, sloped side rails with roller-action handles that slide up and down it to simulate poling. Rather than toe cups to hold your feet, there are thick cushions, so you can exercise in bare feet.

Another interesting advance is that the Fitness Master has adjustable resistance on both the pushing backward and pulling forward motions. It also takes up several less feet of floor space than the NordicTrack. With the side rails removed the Fitness Master is only about 5 inches high and can be slipped under a bed for storage.

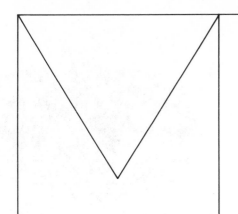

# TRAMPOLINES

One of the most important parts of any exercise program is the "Fun Factor." The more you enjoy your sessions, the more often you'll want to have them. Bouncing around on a trampoline definitely rates high on the fun scale. It's sort of a side benefit that it also happens to be a very healthful activity.

Even though it may look effortless, trampoline jumping, or "aerobic rebounding" as the experts now prefer to call it, really gets your heart and lungs into high gear in short order. As cardiovascular exercise it's up there with stationary bicycling and running on a treadmill. In a study at the University of California at San Diego, women who worked out for 10 weeks on trampolines were found to have reached the same level of fitness as women who exercised for the same amount of time on indoor bikes and treadmills. And in a follow-up study six months later, more of the trampoliners were still sticking with their exercise regimen than the others.

Bouncing this way is what you might call a soft exercise. The spring of the trampoline absorbs a lot of the shock of the action and less impact is transmitted to the bones and joints. Unlike running, very few stress injuries are reported among trampoline users. Trampolines are ideal for older people or anyone suffering from arthritis or back problems.

You can buy full-size trampolines for using out in the yard, but the real hot item today is the mini-trampoline—a scaled-down version for indoors. When not in use, they can be slid neatly into a closet, and some even fold in half for storage.

A good mini-trampoline usually sells for between $50 and $100. Beware of ultra-cheap models selling for $40 or less. They may not hold up under the hours of bouncing you'll want to do. Shop for a trampoline with heavy-duty springs and a frame made of rugged tubing. The shape doesn't matter—some are round and others square—but make sure that the mat is made of polypropylene and not nylon.

Start your bouncing session with a warm-up. You can do some light stretches while sitting on the trampoline, or just jump gently for a few minutes to get your body awake. Then start some vigorous bouncing, preferably to the beat of some lively music. You may find yourself pooping out after a few minutes at first,

but aim eventually to keep yourself at 80 to 85 percent of your maximum heart rate for 20 or 30 minutes.

Occasionally, some users find themselves getting a little dizzy at first. You can buy mini-trampolines with built-in handles, or simply place yours near a wall or heavy chair so you'll have something to grab onto if you lose your balance. And before you get too carried away jumping for joy, make sure your ceiling is high enough.

Naugahyde skirt that covers the springs is available in copper or brown.

### ▶ REBOUND EXERCISER

UNIVERSAL
460 E. 76TH ST.
DENVER, CO 80299
(800) 525-1396

PRICE: $49.95

Universal's mini-trampoline is one of the best around. The frame is rigid 1-inch-square tubing with steel legs that screw in. The springs are connected to the polypropylene mat with a hook and webbing attachment that's stronger than the metal grommets found on cheaper trampolines. The

### ▶ HEXER SIZER

GYM-THING, INC.
5550 NEWBURY ST.
BALTIMORE, MD 21209
(301) 664-0400

PRICE: $99.90
OPTION: T-BAR—$50

The Hexer Sizer is a high-quality, hexagonal mini-trampoline with a welded steel frame, extra-bouncy springs and double-thickness padding around the sides. I particularly like the availability of an optional T-bar handle for balancing yourself when jumping.

### ▶ PACER-MAT

TRI-FLEX MFG., INC.
9191 WINKLER DRIVE,
HOUSTON, TX 77017
(713) 941-3252

PRICE: $169

According to Robert Appel, author of *The Rebound System,* a book on mini-

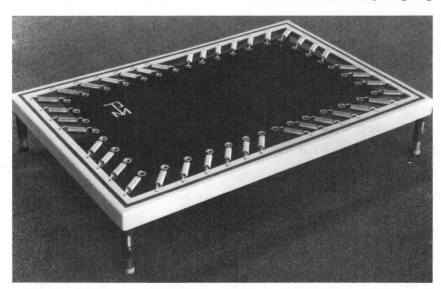

trampolines, square is usually better than round. Appel says many round tramps have a "sweet spot" in the center that's too soft. Square models don't, he says.

In addition to being the right shape, the Pacer-Mat has an extra-thick jumping pad, rugged all-metal frame and heavy-duty springs for extra bounce. The legs are adjustable for height.

### ▶ GALAXY TRAMPOLINE
### Model 442-020

AMF AMERICAN
200 AMERICAN AVE.
JEFFERSON, IA 50129
(800) 247-3978

PRICE: $1,220

This isn't exactly a mini-trampoline, nor can it be used indoors unless you have *very* high ceilings. I like it because it's smaller than some trampolines (9 by 14½ feet), but you can still do some mean acrobatic exercises on it.

The single-thickness polypropylene bed is weather-resistant and is treated to hold up under sunlight. Its 112 cone-shaped springs are galvanized and are attached to the frame with hanger wires for better alignment between springs and frame.

### ▶ REBOUND JOGGING BOARD

GYM-THING, INC.
5550 NEWBURY ST.
BALTIMORE, MD 21209
(301) 664-0401

PRICE: $98.90

This jogging board is much firmer and less bouncy than

a trampoline, but has enough spring to relieve some of the leg and joint trauma of running. It's made of plywood and has a padded running surface and foam inserts to absorb impact. You'll find it somewhat noisier than conventional trampolines.

### ▶ JET-STAR FLYER
#### Model PTN211

THE SHARPER IMAGE
PO BOX 26823
SAN FRANCISCO, CA 94126
(800) 344-4444

PRICE: $127.50 POSTPAID

It's just what it looks like: a space-age pogo stick. Bouncing on this baby can give you a hard aerobic workout while strengthening your knees and leg muscles. The only major difference between this model and the one you used as a kid are the angled, inward-pointing handles that are supposed to be safer. The stick is mostly plastic, with non-slip rubber footrests and a heavy steel spring for plenty of rebound. This might be a great way to get your children interested in exercise.

# INVERSION DEVICES

It all started with Richard Gere dangling like a bat from the ceiling of his high-tech apartment in the movie *American Gigolo.* Before long the switchboards at Paramount were twinkling with thousands of calls from viewers wondering what was up, or rather, down. America became hung up on gravity boots.

Actually, by the time Gere got around to showing off his inverted pectorals, the idea and equipment had already been around for several years. They are the invention of Dr. Robert Martin, a 75-year-old California orthopedist and gravity guru. It's Dr. Martin's theory that the unrelenting force of gravity pushing down on us is responsible for all sorts of physical ills. He says that over the years it compresses our vertebrae, displaces our organs and makes our skin bulge, sag and droop.

The answer to these problems, according to the doctor, is to defy gravity by hanging from your ankles. "In this posture," he says, "the force of gravity upon the body is reversed to a maximum degree [and] all the downward strain produced by an erect posture is relieved. The abdomen draws inward and headward instead of sagging footward and outward. The chest is easily expanded, and the diaphragm is pushed and pulled headward."

Dr. Martin believes that inversion therapy can do

## PUTTING YOUR FEET UP

Once you're in shape, getting your inversion boots hooked onto a door-mounted bar won't be any big deal. But when you first start out, the maneuver can be somewhat intimidating. A length of sturdy rope can make it easier.

1. Tie a non-slipping loop large enough to slip the toe of your shoe into on one end of the rope. Tie the other end to your bar.
2. With your foot in the loop, grab the bar with both hands and shift your weight to the foot in the rope. Hook your free foot onto the bar.
3. Bring your other leg up and hook it. Don't remove the rope.
4. Let go of the bar and hang loose. When you're done, make sure the rope isn't tangled and reverse the procedure. If you can't bend yourself up to grab the bar, use the rope to pull yourself up to it. Unhook the looped foot first, then the other.

everything from easing muscle tension and back pain to curing hemorrhoids. The jury is still out on most of the claims, since there's been almost no scientific testing done on inversion devices. Some doctors think it can be good for you; others say as long as you're healthy to begin with, it can't do much harm.

There's little argument on at least one point, however, among people who use the devices: It's fun. Once you get over the disconcerting sensation of seeing the world topsy-turvy, hanging upside-down is quite relaxing. And at least while you're inverted, minor back and muscle aches do seem to go away.

Being ankles-up also brings a whole new dimension to some familiar exercises. Doing twists, sit-ups, squats or working with weights while inverted uses muscles in a different way—not necessarily better, but different.

If you plan to do some hanging around, the first thing you'll need are the special boots with hooks on the front. Several

companies make them, but they're all basically foam-lined metal bands with ski boot–type clasps. When they originally hit the market, a pair of boots costs nearly $100. Now you can usually find them on sale for a little more than half that.

Once you have the boots, you can hang from an ordinary chin-up bar, provided it's *firmly* anchored to a doorway or suspended from a chain that's properly attached to a wooden ceiling beam. Or you can buy a free-standing metal-pipe frame that has a wide base and a bar on top. Using bars allows lots of freedom to move and exercise in any direction. The only real drawback is that if you're out of shape, getting your feet up to hook the boots onto the bar takes some work.

Although it looks like a futuristic torture device, an oscillation bed makes inverting yourself a lot easier. With this apparatus you can hook your boots to a crossbar while standing up. The padded bed, against which your back and buttocks rest, swings from its middle on an axis, so you can flip yourself upside-down or to any angle you like just by moving your body or arms. To get upright again all you have to do is move your outstretched arms back to your thighs. These beds limit your movement for exercise, but they put less strain on the ankle joints and allow you to choose the angle at which you dangle.

One bit of caution before you run out and buy an inversion device: In at least one university test, using gravity boots seriously elevated the blood pressure of some of the subjects. Apparently their hearts weren't ready for the task of pumping blood *up* to the feet. If you already suffer from even mild hypertension, keep your feet on the ground.

### ▶ *INVERSION BOOTS*

GRAVITY GUIDANCE INC.
150 S. LOS ROBLES AVE.
PASADENA, CA 91101

PRICE: $90

Since you'll be literally trusting your neck to inversion boots, it makes sense to buy a high-quality pair. Gravity Guidance was the first company to make inversion equipment, and they're still the best. Each of these heavy-gauge steel boots weighs about 3 pounds and is lined with a thick layer of neoprene rubber for comfort. The clasp is long and has a narrow angle, so there's almost no chance of it slipping off a bar. One size fits all, but there's extra foam padding supplied for people with small ankles.

### ▶ *INVERSION BOOTS*

GRAVITY GUIDANCE INC.
150 S. LOS ROBLES AVE.
PASADENA, CA 91101

PRICE: $75

These are basically the same boots as the chrome model, but with a sleek, matte black anodized finish instead. The only other significant difference is the price: These are $15 cheaper.

### ▶ *HANG-UPS*

EXERTEC
933 N. INDUSTRIAL PARK DR.
OREM, UT 84057
(800) 453-1194

PRICE: $49

These inversion boots are made of molded urethane plastic instead of metal, which makes them somewhat lighter. They're foam-lined and have a steel buckle.

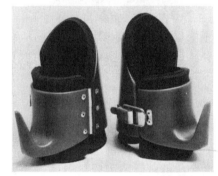

### ▶ *INVERSION BAR*

GRAVITY GUIDANCE INC.
150 S. LOS ROBLES AVE.
PASADENA, CA 91101

PRICE: $25

This 1-inch-diameter chrome-plated steel bar fits into any doorway 30 to 36 inches wide. (Most doors aren't any wider than that.)

Unlike some doorway bars, which are held up by friction or the pressure of a spring inside, this one mounts to the door jamb securely. To install it, screw one of the metal brackets provided to each side of the doorway with four screws. The metal rectangles on the ends of the bar slide snugly into the brackets. Downward pressure from your weight keeps the bar secure during use, but it can be easily removed for storage by simply giving each end a firm tap upward.

### ▶ CHIN-UP BAR

**Model FSCB-28**

JAYFRO
PO BOX 400
WATERFORD, CT 06385
(203) 447-3001

PRICE: $47

The bar is made from 1¼-inch rolled steel welded to ³⁄₁₆-inch-thick, 2-inch-wide plates. The bar can be used for either chin-ups or inversion, provided it's properly secured to the wall. The attachment plates are 32 inches apart, so they should line up with your wall studs.

### ▶ TOGGLE BAR

GRAVITY GUIDANCE INC.
150 S. LOS ROBLES AVE.
PASADENA, CA 91101

PRICE: $49.95

Whatever its benefits might be, inversion therapy by

itself does little for your aerobic fitness and upper-body strength. The Toggle Bar clamps over a bar with a pivot hook so that it can seesaw in either direction. To use it, you grab hold of the ends, bend your legs off the floor, and swing the Toggle Bar up and down. The exercise is sort of a one-arm pull-up that's easier to do than an ordinary chin-up. But it will give you a good workout and stretch your arm, shoulder and back muscles.

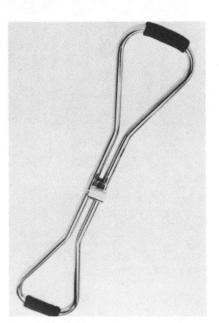

▶ **SKYHOOK**

UNIVERSAL FITNESS
PRODUCTS, INC.
460 E. 76TH AVE.
DENVER, CO 80229
(800) 525-1396

PRICE: $70

The Skyhook is a hybrid inversion device that doesn't require the use of a separate pair of boots. It hooks onto a standard 2-inch bar and has an assist handle below to help you pull yourself up so you can slide your feet into the foam-lined nylon holders. These two-piece adjustable holders have one section that fits over the top of your foot and another that goes just above your heel in the back. The advantages of the Skyhook are mostly a result of its built-in handle. It makes mounting easy and comes in handy for doing pull-up exercises while inverted. A disadvantage is that the mechanism for holding your feet may not leave you feeling as secure when you're upside-down as ankle boots would.

▶ **XER-SISER**

GRAVITY GUIDANCE INC.
150 S. LOS ROBLES AVE.
PASADENA, CA 91101

PRICE: $70

Some taller people may not be able to hang from a standard, inside-the-door-frame bar without their heads coming too close to the floor. This bar solves that problem by extending up and away from the door. It attaches to the inside of a door with brackets that have two height adjustments, and it also rests against the outside of the frame for added support. Unless you are very tall, or do a lot of chin-ups, there may be no need to spend the extra $45 for this bar.

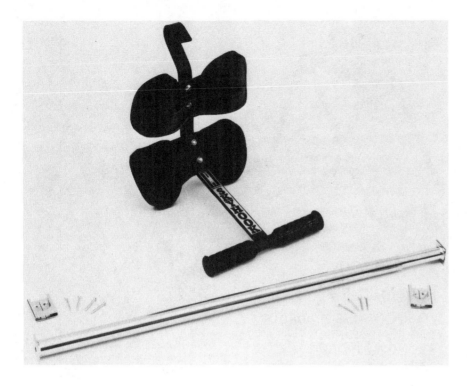

more pressure you are likely to feel on the backs of your ankles, which, essentially, will be supporting most of your weight. One tends to feel less secure than when using ankle boots.

### ▶ *SKYHOOK OSCILLATOR*

UNIVERSAL FITNESS PRODUCTS INC.
460 E. 76TH AVE.,
DENVER, CO 80229
(800)525-1396

PRICE: $249

Like the Skyhook, the Skyhook Oscillator needs no inversion boots. Your feet slide into the built-in holders at the bottom of the device, and your back rests against its flat, plastic bed. By leaning backward, you can swivel your body into a number of positions, from flat out to upside-down. But the steeper the angle, the

### ▸ *BACKSWING*

### *Model Pro II*

BACKSWING CORP.
14351 BONELLI ST.
CITY OF INDUSTRY, CA 91744
(213) 961-0841

PRICE: $350

The Backswing has what amounts to built-in ankle boots. Its two-piece foam-padded leg clamps lock in place under a metal ring. They're quite comfortable and can be adjusted for height. There's a mechanism on the frame that lets you lock yourself into any position, which is a nice feature. The whole unit weighs only 52 pounds and folds for storage.

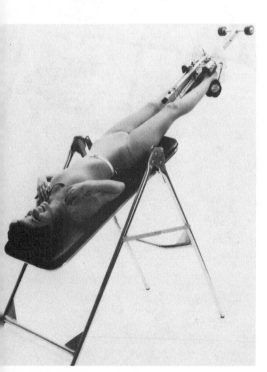

### ▸ *ORTHOPOD*

### *Model GTS100*

MARCY FITNESS PRODUCTS
2801 W. MISSION RD.
ALHAMBRA, CA 91803
(213) 570-1222

PRICE: $360

The Orthopod is a modified inversion device that doesn't require ankle boots. To mount it, you lean the front of your thighs against the large pad and hook your legs around the padded cylinders. Then you can invert yourself by leaning forward. This method puts less stress on ankle and knee joints than boot hanging.

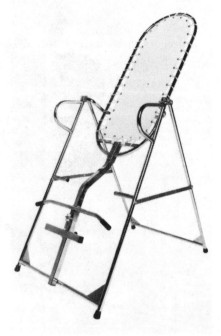

### ▸ *GRAVITY GUIDER*

### *Model 1120*

GRAVITY GUIDANCE INC.
150 LOS ROBLES AVE.
PASADENA, CA 91101

PRICE: $700

The Gravity Guidance 1120 has a comfortable canvas "trampoline" bed and a wider frame than their other models. It's a pleasure to use, but unless you're fanatical about inversion, a much cheaper oscillator will probably suit your needs.

# AEROBIC WEIGHTS

When your car is carrying extra weight it uses more fuel. The same sort of thing happens to your body, and that's the principle behind aerobic weights. By carrying small dumbbells or strapping on weight straps or belts while you exercise, you can burn up more energy and get your heart rate up to your goal in a shorter amount of time.

When doing exercises like running and calisthenics, it's usually the legs that get the best workout since they're moving the weight of the entire body. For most of us, the leg muscles are the ones that are the best developed. They get taxed even when we're just walking around. It's the upper-torso muscles that get shortchanged.

Even some world-class marathon runners are relative weaklings when it comes to upper-body strength.

Aerobic weights can do double duty: making a workout more strenuous while building strength through high-repetition, low-weight exercise. While light weights won't build a lot of muscle bulk, they can improve endurance and power in the arms and chest.

Leonard Schwartz, a Pittsburgh psychiatrist, has written an entire book on aerobic weights, *Heavyhands*. He says that arms and legs working together can perform longer than legs alone at the same work intensity and that exercise feels more comfortable with all the limbs working in combination. And pound-for-pound, he continues, arm muscles consume more oxygen during exercise than leg muscles.

Two of Dr. Schwartz's favored aerobic weight exercises are called "pump 'n' walk" and "pump 'n' run." As the names imply, the idea is to walk or jog while pumping weighted arms alternately up and down.

One-piece dumbbells can be used for these exercises, provided the handle-width is short. But this really isn't ideal equipment. You can get hand cramps from gripping the weights too tightly, and can bonk yourself or a passerby if you don't grip them tightly enough.

Special weights for aerobics are now being sold. One of the most popular, named after Dr. Schwartz's book, has a snug-fitting bar over the dumbbell handle to ensure a firm hold. In addition, there are weighted gloves (usually weighing about a pound each) and soft plastic strap-on wrist bracelets. If

you want to get a feel for aerobic hand weights without spending much money, just fill a pair of tightly-woven socks with sand or BBs and run with one in each hand.

For building legs up there are also ankle weights and even some that tie onto the laces of running shoes. For safety's sake you should probably avoid using more than 2½ pounds per leg. Heavier weights may throw your gait off and cause a fall.

Many athletes find that wearing aerobic weights in a vest or belt is the most comfortable. Some belts and vests come with pockets to hold individual lead weights, others are made of plastic foam with the weights built-in. Again, it's not wise to run around carrying a load of more than 3 percent of your body weight. Better to increase the length or intensity of your exercise than to load up on extra poundage.

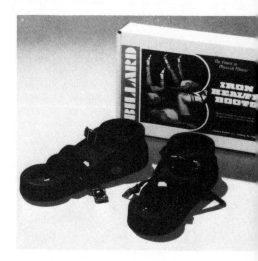

### ▸ IRON HEALTH BOOTS
### Model IHB

BILLARD BARBELL CO.
208 CHESNUT ST.
READING, PA 19602
(215) 375-4333

PRICE: $9.50

It might be stretching just a little to call these aerobic weights; they're more for building up hips, legs and knees. The boots weigh about 7½ pounds each and have holes on the sides through which you can slide a dumbbell bar to add more weight. Used alone they make passable aerobic weights for floor exercises.

### ▸ AEROBIC HANDWEIGHTS

DIVAJEX
15551 REDHILL AVE.
TUSTIN, CA 92680
(714) 832-8970

PRICE: $15

### ▶ LACE WEIGHTS

AMF WHITELY
29 ESSEX ST.
MAYWOOD, NJ 07607
(201) 843-3210

PRICE: $19.95

Some people are bothered because ankle weights slide around on their legs too much and throw off their stride. AMF's Lace Weights solve that problem because they thread onto the shoelaces of running shoes and have a Velcro strap that holds them securely in place. Pouches on the sides hold packets of lead pellets that let you vary the weight from $\frac{1}{2}$ pound to $2\frac{1}{2}$ pounds per foot.

If you use these, remember to put equal amounts of weight on each foot and build up slowly to the maximum $2\frac{1}{2}$ pounds.

### ▶ WRIST/ANKLE WEIGHTS
### Model FSEW-17

JAYFRO CORP.
976 HARTFORD TPKE.
WATERFORD, CT 06385
(203) 447-3001

PRICE: $34 (PAIR)

Each of these soft foam weights has 2 pounds of weight inside. They fasten on your ankles or wrists with Velcro and are adjustable. This type of weight is bulky but comfortable.

These hand weights weigh 1 pound each and have a Velcro wrist fastener and straps to slide your fingers through. They stay put and feel quite comfortable.

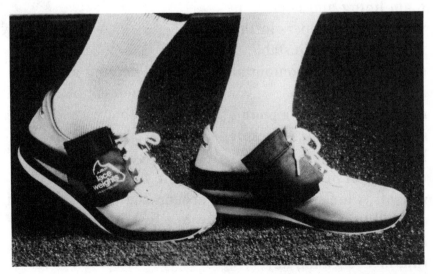

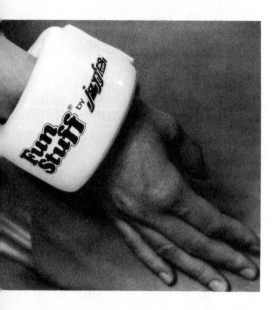

### ▶ *WEIGHTED VEST*

LOGJAMMER INDUSTRIES
332 WATER ST.
KEENE, NH 03431
(603) 325-5608

PRICE: $69.95

Vests can be a comfortable way to wear aerobic weights. This one is made of bright yellow canvas with foam lining and is machine washable. It zippers in the front and has adjustable side straps. The contoured steel weights, each weighing just over a pound, slip into individual pockets in front and back. It comes with a total of 50 pounds of weights, which seems like overkill to me. I can't imagine anyone wanting to run, or even walk, any distance hauling around an extra 30 percent or more of his or her body weight, and I don't recommend it. You should try to place the weight you do use evenly around the vest so that you won't feel off-balance.

# JUMP ROPES

Adults are rediscovering the jump rope. It's not only women either—busy executives have taken to carrying them in their briefcases for a handy fitness break at work. Sporting goods stores report that they sell more jump ropes now than ever before. And a few years ago, a gym in New York offered a 6-week course in rope jumping.

One thing you've got to give them credit for—they're cheap. A top-of-the-line model complete with a digital counter will only set you back about $15. Even a length of clothesline will get the job done, although something with a few more refinements will make things easier. Look for a jump rope that offers some system to keep it from constantly tangling around your feet. On some models this is accomplished with plastic discs or tubes that slide along the rope and keep it weighted at the bottom. Others have handles with ball bearings inside to keep things unsnarled. The one I use has weighted wooden handles with ball bearings and a heavy leather rope. It has never tripped me up.

Make sure that the jump rope you buy is the right size. A rope for someone who's 6 feet 2 inches tall won't do at all for someone who's 5 feet 1 inch. For a perfect fit, the rope should stretch from armpit to armpit while you're standing on it with both feet.

Forget the old playground image. Skipping rope is good for you. It can help develop greater leg and knee strength, jumping ability, and faster running speed, as well as improve agility and flexibility. And it gives the cardiovascular system a real going over.

Be careful, though. Jump ropes are serious equipment. A few minutes of the old double-dutch can shoot your heart rate into the red zone. Few people can sustain the activity for 20 or 30 seconds at a time when they're out of shape.

Doctors who studied jumping rope at Ball State University in Indiana say you ought to be capable of walking a brisk 3 miles without tiring before you even *think* about taking out the jump rope. After that it's still advisable to start slowly. Try 20-second sessions followed by an equal spell of rest. Begin with six of these sessions and work your way up slowly to a total of 5 or 10 minutes a day.

The great thing about working out with a jump rope is that you don't have to worry about what to do with it when you're done. Just hang it over the nearest door knob until tomorrow.

### ▶ *JUMP ROPE*

#### *Model PR*

ARISTO IMPORTS CO.
15 HUNT RD.
ORANGEBURG, NY 10962
(914) 359-0720

PRICE: $3.30

This is your basic, no-frills jump rope with an 8-foot woven cotton cord and wooden handles.

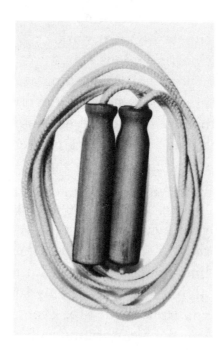

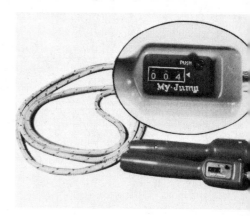

### ▶ *DIGITAL JUMP ROPE*

#### *Model DR*

ARISTO IMPORTS CO.
15 HUNT RD.
ORANGEBURG, NY 10962
(914) 359-0720

PRICE: $9.95

The counter in one of the plastic handles of this 8-foot jump rope keeps track of up to 999 skips. It has ball bearings in the handles and a sliding vinyl tube to weight down the bottom of the rope and prevent it from wearing as it hits the floor.

### ▶ *LIFELINE JUMP ROPE*

#### *Model LJR 4*

LIFELINE
1421 S. PARK ST.
MADISON, WI 53715
(800) 356-9607

PRICE: $11.95

The colored plastic cylinders covering this

jump rope aren't just for show. Their weight helps balance the rope and prevent tangling. If you want to, you can really get this thing flying! It's adjustable and has a mechanical digital counter to keep track of the revolutions. The company makes a similar jump rope (Model LJR 5) with foam-padded handles and no counter. It sells for $9.95. Both come with a 40-page booklet on jump rope exercises.

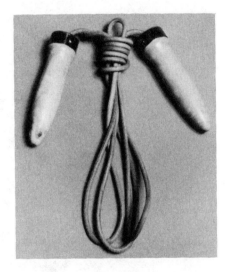

### ▶ LEATHER JUMP ROPE
#### Model 07162

JAYFRO CORP.
976 HARTFORD TPKE.
WATERFORD, CT 06385
(203) 447-3001

PRICE: $13.50

The 90-inch rope is made of leather for weight, and

there are ball bearings in the wooden handles to keep it from getting snarled. This is a very smooth jump rope.

### ▶ JUMP STARS

GYM-THING, INC.
5550 NEWBURY ST.
BALTIMORE, MD 21209
(301) 664-0401

PRICE: $23.90

For a jump rope, this European model is quite complex. It features an easily adjustable 7⅞-foot-long nylon-core rope and long, plastic handles. Up to a pound of screw-on weights can be added to each handle, as can a skip counter and calorie meter.

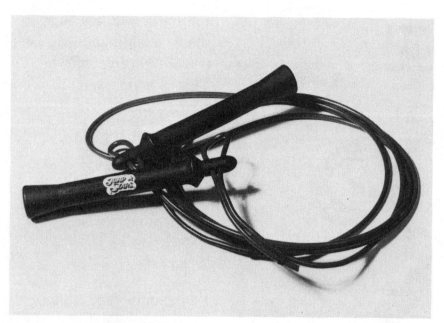

## ▶ *JUMPERCISER*

JUMPERCISER
1986 EAST 3RD ST.
BROOKLYN, NY 11223
(212) 339-2204

PRICE: $24.95

What makes this jump rope different are weighted handles to give your upper body more of a workout. It has a 10-foot nylon cord, ball-bearing action and soft foam grips.

# METERS AND MONITORS

When you exercise regularly, there's no better morale booster than some tangible evidence of improvement—a shred of proof, no matter how small, that all this work is doing some good. The payoff may come in being able to run or pedal an extra mile without tiring, or lifting a barbell more times than you could the week before. I've seen friends act as excited and proud at one of these small victories as they did when their baby took its first step.

Be assured that for every external measure of progress there are several more improvements that aren't as evident. For instance, if you don't keep track of your resting pulse rate, you may not see it creeping steadily downward as your heart becomes stronger and more efficient. But that might be the very reason why you can exercise longer and harder now than you could last month.

Getting to know your pulse can also help you design a fitness program that works fast. Exercise physiologists say working your heart rate up to 70 to 80 percent of its maximum (your age subtracted from the number 220) and keeping it there for 20 or 30 minutes a session is the quickest road to cardiovascular improvement.

Measuring your resting pulse by hand is a fine way to keep a weekly heart-rate log. In fact, a study at Southern Illinois University found that monitoring your pulse by hand can provide a reading as accurate as that of an expensive electrocardiogram machine.

Some people have a hard time finding and counting their pulse. And it's a bother to try counting your pulse in the middle of a workout to see if you've reached your target rate. In these cases, an electric pulse meter may come in handy. These small computers range in price from $60 to well over $200. Some slip over a finger, others have a wired sensor that's clipped to your earlobe, and a few of the more expensive models are attached to a belt that fits around your chest.

But are they accurate? Sometimes. *Bicycling* magazine found that the models they tested compared favorably with a local hospital's EKG unit—*if* the user stayed reasonably still. But when their volunteers wiggled around on a stationary bike seat or moved a finger, some meters gave readings that fluctuated by as much as 60 beats.

In my own more informal testing, I found that monitors with an ear clip or chest strap seemed to be affected the least by movement. You should try a few units out yourself before you choose one to buy.

Another good measure of fitness is the maximum volume of oxygen your body consumes during exercise, known as your $VO_2$ *max.* The more fit you get, the more oxygen your body is able to process. There aren't any home measuring devices for $VO_2$ yet, but a doctor can test yours for you. According to Drs. Arthur Weltman and Bryant Stamford of the University of Kentucky, a good rule of thumb is to figure that in early training your $VO_2$ max will improve 10 to 20 percent after 10 weeks of vigorous exercise.

Currently there's one home device on the market, and probably more on the way, that measures your lung capacity. But since the amount of air your lungs hold changes little even after lots of exercise (it's the volume of oxygen that they can utilize that

improves), this type of monitor has limited use.

Numerous tests have shown that regular exercise can lower blood pressure. If you suffer from hypertension, I think it's worthwhile to keep one of the new electric blood pressure monitors in your home gym. You'll find them simple to use: The most you have to do is slip the cuff around your arm and press a button. A tiny compressor in the base will automatically inflate the cuff and read your blood pressure. Many measure your pulse, too, and some even print out a little paper strip like an adding machine. Don't expect a major change in blood pressure overnight. Rather, look for a slow decline, with occasional blips after a hectic day.

▶ *PULSE WATCH*
*Model S33-160*

EDMUND SCIENTIFIC CO.
101 E. GLOUSTER PIKE
BARRINGTON, NJ 08007
(800) 232-6677

PRICE: $59.95

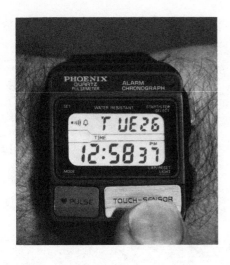

This digital watch has all the usual features—calendar, alarm, chronograph and stopwatch functions—plus a built-in pulse monitor. To get a readout you just put your finger on the sensor and wait until the readout stops counting. Accuracy of the time mechanism, but not the pulse monitor, is guaranteed.

#### ▶ *HEALTHCHEK*

TIMEX MEDICAL PRODUCTS
WATERBURY, CT 06720
(800) 643-4444

PRICE: $70

The Timex blood pressure monitor is about as foolproof as they come. It's entirely automatic—all you do is slip on the cuff and push a button. Full

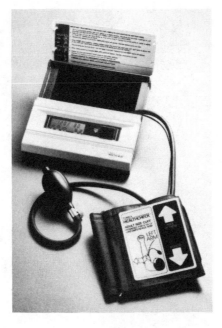

instructions are printed on the lid, and there's even a little indicator that flashes if something has gone wrong and the reading is incorrect. When the University of Alabama School of Medicine tested this machine they found it nearly as accurate as the manual cuff that doctors use.

#### ▶ *THE WINDMILL*

KINETIX
118 ROUTE 17 NORTH
UPPER SADDLE RIVER, NJ
07458
(800) 356-9607

PRICE: $88

The Windmill is a handheld device for measuring the volume of air you take into your lungs with each breath. It has a replaceable mouthpiece and four-digit mechanical counter. If you're a recently reformed smoker, or have just started training after years of inactivity, you may see a small increase in lung volume after exercising, according to an article on The Windmill in *American Health* magazine. But, as the writer points out, the increase may be too small to make this a good device to motivate you to exercise. The real change will come in the amount of oxygen your body *uses,* a factor not measured by The Windmill.

### ▶ AMEREC 130

#### Model DM 130

AMEREC CORP.
PO BOX 3825
BELLEVUE, WA 98009
(800) 426-0858

PRICE: $125

A simple, handlebar-mounted monitor for cyclists and treadmill joggers, the Amerec 130 uses an ear sensor and measures both heart rate and elapsed time.

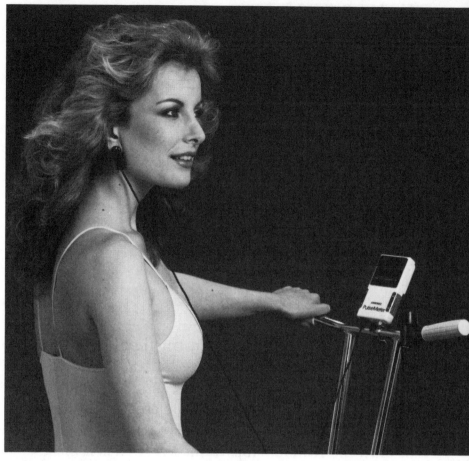

### ▶ PULSEMETER

#### Model PM110

AMEREC
PO BOX 3825
BELLEVUE, WA 98009
(800) 426-0858

PRICE: $139

The Pulsemeter can be mounted on the handlebars of a stationary bike or the side rails of a treadmill or clipped to your belt. It uses a clothespin-type sensor that you attach to your ear lobe. The meter displays your heartbeat in digits and with a light that blinks with each pulse. It also doubles as a stopwatch with hour/minute and minute/second modes. Battery life is about 9 hours.

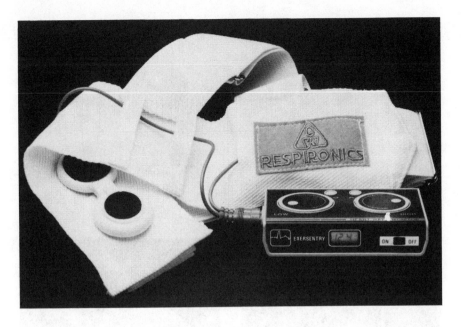

## ▶ EXERSENTRY
### Model EX-3

RESPIRONICS, INC.
650 SECO RD.
MONROEVILLE, PA 15146
(412) 373-8114

PRICE: $170
OPTIONS: BIKE/TREADMILL
      MOUNT—$8.95
      BELT CLIP—$4

The Exersentry heart-rate monitor is worn in a chest belt and has two electrode sensors that measure your pulse directly. You can move around all you like and the reading won't be affected. The card deck–size monitor has a digital readout and an audio signal that warns you when you've exceeded, or fallen below, your pre-set target heart rate. For use with a treadmill or stationary bike, the monitor slips out of its pocket on the belt and mounts on the handlebars.

## ▶ THE COACH
### Model S33-106

EDMUND SCIENTIFIC
101 E. GLOUSTER PIKE
BARRINGTON, NJ 08007
(800) 232-6677

PRICE: $199.95
OPTION: BICYCLE
      ADAPTER—$29.95

Although it weighs just 3 ounces and is about the size of a bar of soap, The Coach is a fairly sophisticated fitness computer. When you wear it jogging, it measures your distance, calories burned, number of strides, average speed and elapsed time. And when you don the chest strap, it measures heart rate and will beep when you exceed your pre-set target pulse. You can program it to your needs by punching in data on your sex, age, weight and resting and target maximum heart rate.

An adapter kit makes it possible to use The Coach on a regular or stationary bike (you program in the wheel circumference so it can measure distance traveled). When *Bicycling* magazine tested it on a bike they found the Velcro fasteners a bit of a nuisance and complained that the readout was difficult for some riders to see when the unit was mounted on the handlebars.

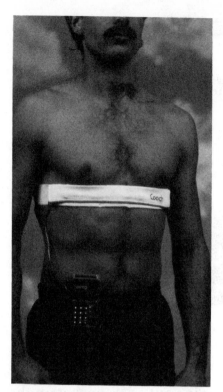
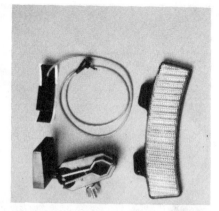
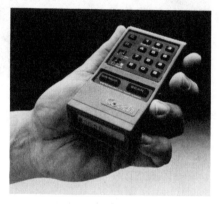

# GRIP STRENGTH-ENERS

They say a handshake tells a lot about a person. At the very least it'll tip you off to how good his tennis game is. A powerful grip is an asset if you play racquet sports, baseball or football. If you're planning an exercise program around free weights, strengthening your grip will help you control the barbell better. And as most golfers know, working on a strong grip can shave strokes off your game.

Actually, a steely grip involves much more than just hand muscles. It's the muscles of the wrist and forearm that give much of the power to your grasp.

Some professional athletes use machines costing $2,000 or more that do nothing but improve their grasp. These devices usually have a stationary bar to rest the palm against and a movable finger bar connected to a pulley and weight stack. Few of us need to be *that* concerned about a firm handshake.

Luckily there are lots of inexpensive gadgets around which are more than adequate for those of us who don't make a living playing sports. The one you're probably most familiar with is the simple spring grip. It has two contoured plastic handles connected by a heavy coiled spring and usually sells for less than $5. Most of these that I've tried in the past were too wide for my hands and too difficult to squeeze.

Luckily some manufacturers have since caught onto the fact that we're not all Arnold Schwarzenegger and are making smaller models with less resistance.

Grips made of sponge rubber about the size of a bar of soap are a newer wrinkle. Several of those I've tested were so soft I could squeeze them tightly without so much as a bulging forearm muscle. Only the most rigid ones offered enough resistance to make me feel like I was getting any benefit.

Before you buy any grip strengthener, take it out of the box and use it for a minute or two. You should be able to feel your muscles working all the way up to the shoulder. If you can squeeze it more than 10 times without tiring, you either have a strong enough grip already or the device is too soft.

I keep my favorite hand grip—a small spring model with curved handles—in the glove compartment of my car. When I get stuck in a traffic jam I pull it out to give me something to work my frustration out on. It

keeps my blood pressure down and has done wonders for my racquetball game.

▶ *WOODEN HAND GRIPS*
*Model 414*

LECO INTERNATIONAL
48 BURD ST.
NYACK, NY 10960
(914) 358-6770

PRICE: $2.80

These are inexpensive wooden grips with seven zinc-chrome springs. They come in black, red and natural. You must be careful not to pinch your skin with these.

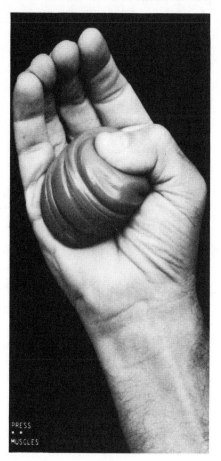

▶ *POWER PUTTY*

SPORTSHEALTH PRODUCTS
527 W. WINDSOR RD.
GLENDALE, CA 91204

PRICE: $6.50

It may look silly, but Power Putty isn't kid-stuff. Squeezing and pulling it can help build stronger, more dexterous hand and finger muscles. According to *Golf Illustrated* magazine, orthopedic surgeon and former UCLA football team physician Robert Watanbe

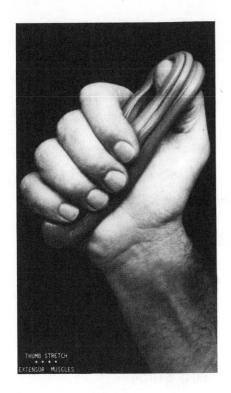

THUMB STRETCH
★ ★ ★ ★
EXTENSOR MUSCLES

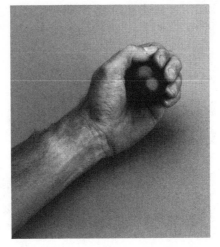

recommends Power Putty for prevention of tennis elbow and as therapy for arthritis sufferers.

The putty is actually a non-toxic silicone polymer that's dense enough to produce resistance but pliable enough to mold into a variety of shapes. You can roll it into a ball to squeeze or wrap it around your thumb to do muscle stretches, among other things. You might even catch yourself having fun with it. And no, it doesn't come packaged in a little plastic egg.

### ▶ GRIP STRENGTHENER

### Model Y31-662

EDMUND SCIENTIFIC
101 E. GLOUSTER PIKE
BARRINGTON, NJ 08007
(800) 232-6677

PRICE: $6.95

Edmund's grip strengthener is a black ball made from a rubber-like material called *sorbothane.* You can squeeze it with your hands to develop wrist and forearm, or grip it with your feet to strengthen toes and instep.

### ▶ WRIST ROLL-UP

### Model WR

BILLARD BARBELL CO.
208 CHESNUT ST.
READING, PA 19602
(215) 375-4333

PRICE: $8

The idea is to twist the rope around the bar to lift the 5-pound weight. It develops the wrists, hands and forearms. You might try making your own version with a dumbbell bar and some strong nylon cord.

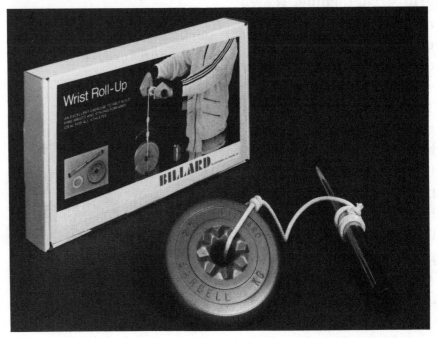

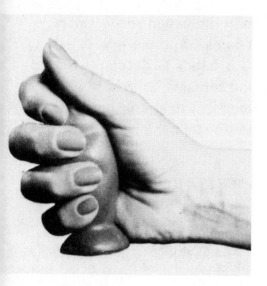

### ▶ GRIP-X

ALIMED, INC.
68 HARRISON AVE.
BOSTON, MA 02111
(617) 451-2240

PRICE: $9.95

The Grip-X exerciser was developed by a doctor for injury rehabilitation and grip strengthening. It's made of rubber and has a unique shape that's comfortable to use and that supports the finger joints. The Grip-X comes in three grades: soft, medium and hard. I'd only recommend the soft model if you're trying to get an injured hand back in shape. Otherwise it doesn't provide enough resistance. The medium model is best for most people.

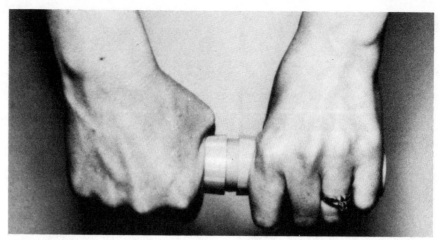

### ▶ EXER-TWIST

MADDAK, INC.
PEQUANNOCK, NJ 07440
(201) 694-0500

PRICE: $10

The Exer-Twist is rare among hand/wrist exercisers in that it has adjustable resistance. This is a twisting exercise—something like wringing out a wet towel—and it's particularly good for the wrists and forearms.

### ▶ MY-GRIPPER

#### Model MG

ARISTO IMPORT CO.
15 HUNT RD.
ORANGEBURG, NY 10962
(914) 359-0720

PRICE: $24.50

Billed as the "world's first digital hand strengthener," the My-Gripper has a mechanical 1 through 999 squeeze counter and meter that tells you how many pounds of force you're exerting. It's made of hard plastic and is compact enough to fit small hands.

# PORTABLE POWER

A business trip or long vacation is no time to leave your exercise program behind. Two weeks of stress and steak bernaise without a little exercise once in a while can really derail a fitness schedule. But if you can at least keep your system cranked up with moderate exercise while you're on the road, you'll return home feeling better and won't have to work nearly as hard to get back into shape.

To their credit, many large hotel chains, among them the Sheraton, Marriott and Hyatt, are recognizing that their guests are concerned about staying healthy and have installed gyms in some of their properties. The hotel health clubs I've used have been consistently first-rate, with quality equipment, whirlpools, saunas and even an occasional masseuse on duty. One California Hyatt hotel goes so far as to offer aerobic room service. They'll equip your room with a stationary bike or treadmill for a small service charge.

Some hotels are slow in catching on, and I still find myself, more often than I'd like, staying someplace where the owner's idea of healthful accommodations is a "Magic Fingers" bed. Those are the times when I'm glad I thought to pack one of my portable exercise gadgets before I left.

Most of the equipment in this chapter is small enough to slip into an overnighter or briefcase. These are not complicated machines, and I wouldn't recommend any of them for everyday use. But they can help you maintain your present fitness level for a week or two until you get back to your home gym.

Don't leave home without one.

### ▶ CHEST EXPANDERS

#### Models 310, 311 and 313

LECO INTERNATIONAL
48 BURD ST.
NYACK, NY 10960
(914) 358-6770

PRICES: 3-SPRING—$6.40
4-SPRING—$6.80
5-SPRING—$7.60

I bought my first chest expander when I was about 12, hoping it would give me a bulging chest like those guys in the comic book ads. It didn't, but I had fun trying and dreaming.

Actually, these devices can tone chest and arm muscles some. Springs are removable to modify them to your strength level. Let me share a lesson I learned soon after I bought one: Don't hold it too close to your chest, or you'll get a nasty pinch. Another alternative is to buy the

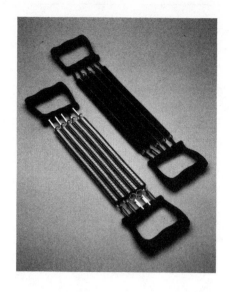

model with rubber cords instead of springs.

### ▶ POWER TWISTERS

#### Models 318–323

LECO INTERNATIONAL
48 BURD ST.
NYACK, NY 10960
(914) 358-6770

PRICE: $13

This simple device—two handles connected by a

heavy spring—is meant to exercise the arms and shoulders. You can twist it upwards, downwards or radially to work different muscle groups. There's no way to increase the tension, so the gain is finite.

### ▶ WEDG-IT

H. WESLEY & CO.
PO BOX 10496
HARRISBURG, PA 17105

PRICE: $10.20 POSTPAID

Here's a clever little device for holding your feet down when you do sit-ups. The rubber wedge slides under a door or piece of furniture while the nylon strap and Velcro closure hold your ankles or feet in place. It can be used for bent and straight-leg sit-ups.

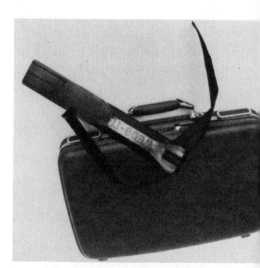

### ▸ PORTA-GYM

PORTA-GYM PRODUCTS
PO BOX 1751
BLOOMINGTON, IL 61701

PRICE: $16.95 POSTPAID

This travel kit contains a jump rope and a looped elastic cord for stretching exercises. The plastic tube they come in can be filled with water and used as a dumbbell.

### ▸ QUICK TRIM SYSTEM
#### Model 619

LECO INTERNATIONAL
48 BURD ST.
NYACK, NY 10960
(914) 358-6770

PRICE: $20

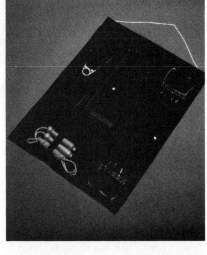

The Quick Trim System is a roll-up travel kit that contains a jump rope, grip strengthener, four-spring chest expander and something the company calls a ''tension rower''—a single heavy spring with a handle on one end and covered foot holders on the other—a sort of miniature rowing machine.

### ▶ SIT-UP BAR

#### Model 31965

EDMUND SCIENTIFIC
101 E. GLOUSTER PIKE
BARRINGTON, NJ 08007
(800) 257-6173

PRICE: $16.95

This 12-inch bar clamps around the bottom of a door to hold your feet in place for sit-ups. I'd like it better if the bar had some padding, but it's still a handy gadget.

### ▶ GRIPPER

#### Model GRP

AMF AMERICAN
200 AMERICAN AVE.
JEFFERSON, IA 50129
(800) 247-3978

PRICE: $25

This two-way exercise bar can be used for pulling exercises on one end and pushing ones on the other. It has four steel springs for tension, any of which can be removed to change the resistance. The range of motion with devices like this is somewhat limited,

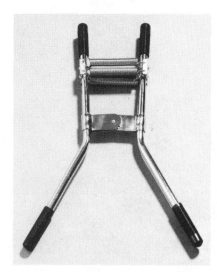

and so, therefore, is the benefit derived.

### ▶ LIFELINE GYM

#### Model LG1

KINETIX
118 RT. 17 NORTH
UPPER SADDLE RIVER, NJ
07458
(800) 431-1662

PRICE: $39.95

The Lifeline Gym is small enough to fit into an attaché case but versatile enough to be included as an accessory on one of Universal's $3,000-plus circuit training machines.

The basic parts of this compact system are a length of stretchy tubing with a handle on each end, and a snap-together plastic bar with a trough running down its length to hold the tubing in place. You can put one handle over each foot and lift the bar or stand on the bar and pull on the handles. The kit also comes with a clever attachment that allows you to use it for resistance while you run in place. It consists of a wide belt that slips through the handles and around your waist and a plastic clip that you shut in

▶ *TRAVEL WEIGHTS*
### *Model S33-374*

EDMUND SCIENTIFIC
101 E. GLOUSTER PIKE
BARRINGTON, NJ 08007
(800) 232-6677

PRICE: $39.95

I call these "instant dumbbells." Just add water. The plastic canisters have locking plugs so when you fill them with water, they won't leak. When full they each weigh 5 pounds. The bar is also plastic and the weights lock onto it with a pin. Travel Weights come with six canisters, a bar and a black duffel bag for carrying. You'll need two sets if you want to do exercises using both arms at once.

a door jamb. The clip holds one end of the tubing tight while you stretch against the other end and "run." Strange as it sounds, this feature works effectively. You can change the amount of resistance easily for most of the exercises by simply wrapping some of the tubing around the handle.

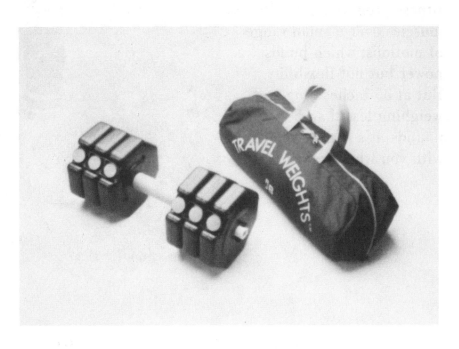

# ▶ BULLWORKER

## *Model 33531*

EDMUND SCIENTIFIC
101 E. GLOUSTER PIKE
BARRINGTON, NJ 08007
(800) 257-6173

PRICE: $49

The Bullworker is a very popular strength-building device that mainly benefits the arms and chest. It's made of a small cylinder that slides into a larger one with a spring inside for resistance. Your job is to push the two handles together against the spring. There are also plastic-wrapped steel cords on the sides for doing pulling exercises.

I think the Bullworker is of limited use in an overall fitness program. It works muscles over a small range of motions, which builds power but not flexibility. But at 35 inches long and weighing less than 5 pounds, it's handy to take with you when traveling.

# AFTER THE WORKOUT . . .

The part of every workout I like best is the end. As the old punch line goes: It feels so good when I stop. I seem to relax better after exercise. An exercise physiologist might explain that I feel that way because I've worked some of the tension out of my muscles and stimulated calming brain chemicals known as endorphins. But just as important, I think, is the feeling that I've *earned* my rest.

I'm always looking for a way to prolong that post-exercise glow. The warm, bubbling massage of a whirlpool bath is about the closest I've been able to come to it. After 20 minutes of being pounded by a jet stream of air and water, I'm jelly. There's not a great deal of evidence that whirlpools are therapeutic for most people, but who cares when it feels that good?

Owning your own whirlpool is cheaper than it used to be but still remains an expensive luxury. The lowest-priced bathtub-sized units cost between $1,000 and $1,500. But if you're building a new house or remodeling an old bathroom, it's worth considering.

Some people prefer relaxing in a hot sauna after a workout. Sweating in the 95- to 100-degree heat of a sauna for 15 minutes or so leaves you feeling clean and relaxed. There's even some evidence that it can temporarily lower blood pressure and increase blood circulation to the skin. Claims of any significant long-term health benefits, however, are mostly mythical. Saunas won't help you lose weight, condition your heart or force your body to sweat out pollutants.

Kits with all the parts for building a one-person redwood sauna cost about $1,500, heater included. The parts are all pre-cut, and if you're handy, you can probably put one together in a weekend. Larger saunas that accommodate two or more people run in the $2,000 to $3,000 range.

Sore muscles can sometimes put a damper on whatever little party you throw for yourself after a workout. Frequently the pain doesn't start until the next day, but occasionally you'll feel it right away. A little stiffness is natural when you've just begun an exercise program, but if you really throb, chances are that some of the tiny fibers that make up muscle tissue have been torn.

The best remedy is still a little dab of Ben-Gay or other deep-heat lotion rubbed into the sore area. If it's not too tender, a light massage with an electric vibrator like those mentioned in this chapter can help.

### ▶ FOOT BATH
#### Model F-140H

POLLENEX
111 N. CANAL ST.
CHICAGO, IL 60606
(312) 454-5400

PRICE: $39.95

After a tough workout you can slip out of your sweaty sneakers and into this vibrating foot bath that will also heat the water if you want. It's addicting.

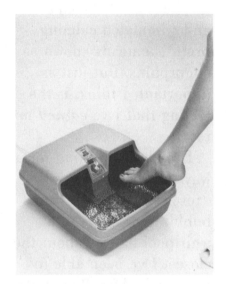

### ▶ SWEDISH-STYLE MASSAGER

OSTER
5055 N. LYDELL AVE.
MILWAUKEE, WI 53217
(414) 332-8300

PRICE: $62

You supply the hand, the machine provides the vibration. It clamps onto your hand with two sets of narrow springs and has intensity settings from "gentle" to "vigorous."

### ▶ NOVAFON SONIC MASSAGER

### Model PER801

THE SHARPER IMAGE
PO BOX 26823
SAN FRANCISCO, CA 94126
(800) 344-4444

PRICE: $154.50 POSTPAID

Instead of the usual vibrating head, the Novafon uses sound waves—emitted at 10,000 pulses per second—to massage muscles. The company that sells it claims the machine can stimulate blood circulation 2¼ inches beneath the skin. The light metal, hand-held massager comes with two washable heads, one flat, the other rounded, and a cord that extends to 7 feet.

### ▶ DEEP HEAT BACK MASSAGER

### Model B-400

POLLENEX
111 N. CANAL
CHICAGO, IL 60606
(312) 454-5400

PRICE: $49.95

For soothing sore muscles, this washable vinyl pad offers both infra-red heat and vibrating massage. The rounded portion moves on a Velcro track so that you can position it to concentrate the heat and massage where they're needed.

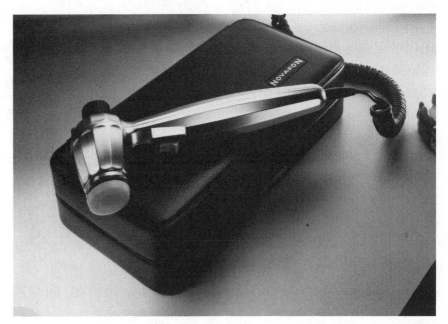

### ▶ AMEREC STEAMER

#### Model AR50

AMEREC
PO BOX 3825
BELLEVUE, WA 98009
(800) 426-0858

PRICE: $590

This 5,000-watt steamer turns your bathroom or shower enclosure into a steam room. It's self-contained and requires no filters, pumps or chemicals. All that shows once it's installed (you'll need a plumber to do that) is the chrome outlet head. The company also makes pre-cut cedar kits (including heater) beginning at $1,520 for a 4-by-4-foot room.

### ▶ STEAM/SAUNA BATH

#### Model SA2-ABS

VITAMASTER INDUSTRIES
455 SMITH ST.
BROOKLYN, NY 11231
(212) 858-0505

PRICE: $695

You don't even need a plumber to install this steam/sauna unit. All you have to do is plug it in. The molded plastic body has a heating unit built into the space under the seat to supply dry heat or steam. The water reservoir holds 2 quarts, enough for about 1½ hours of wet heat. The

*Ultramaster*

heater, which operates on 120-volt service, has a thermostat control and a timer that will shut it off after a pre-set interval.

The total weight of the unit is 77 pounds. There is a set of wheels at the back so it can be moved easily.

▶ *ACU-MASSAGE TABLE*

*Model FL*

H.W.E., INC.
1638 N. LA BREA AVE.
LOS ANGELES, CA 90028
(213) 466-8400

PRICE: $1,795

Before I tried the Acu-Massage Table, I was expecting just another vibrating mattress like you find in motel rooms. Then I laid down, switched it on, and got my mind changed. When the timer shut it down 15 minutes later, they practically had to drag me off.

The 6½-by-2-foot table doesn't vibrate at all, it actually gives you a massage. Two sets of knobby rubber rollers on axles run up and down tracks underneath the pad. The track has high and low spots that follow the curve of your spine. The sensation is one of a slow-moving wave of fingers rubbing you down from head to foot. Laying directly on the pad gives quite an intense massage. The table comes with another thicker pad that you can add if you want an easier rubdown. There are also two vinyl-covered sandbags included to concentrate the massage on the backs of your legs.

The Acu-Massage can be operated manually, or it can be set to shut off automatically with its mechanical timer. (The manufacturer recommends that it be used no longer than 15 minutes per day.)

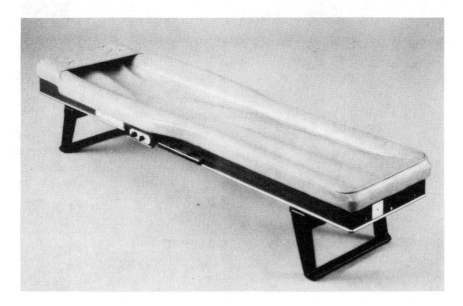

If you don't mind taking your whirlpool baths alone, this Jacuzzi model has the advantage of being sized to fit in the same space as most standard bathtubs. It's 30 inches deep and has a contoured seat and reclining backrest. There are three adjustable whirlpool jets. The tub comes pre-plumbed from the factory, so installation is fairly simple.

### ▶ *THE ESPREE*

JACUZZI WHIRLPOOL BATH
298 N. WIGET LANE
WALNUT CREEK, CA 94596
(800) 227-0710

PRICE: $2,195

This 28-inch-deep whirlpool seats four and is portable. All you have to do is plug it in and fill it—a heater and filter are built in.

### ▶ *THE LUSSO*

JACUZZI WHIRLPOOL BATH
298 N. WIGET LANE
WALNUT CREEK, CA 94596
(800) 227-0710

PRICE: $2,400

## ▶ *THE ADONIS*

JACUZZI WHIRLPOOL BATH
298 N. WIGET LANE
WALNUT CREEK, CA 94596
(800) 227-0710

PRICE: $2,550

An intimate tub for two, Jacuzzi's Adonis is 4-by-5 feet and 23 inches deep. There are four whirlpool jets, one in each corner. A single control console adjusts temperature and jet intensity. The tub can be sunk flush with the floor, as shown, or stand on its own above floor level.